Praise for

Mike Krebill and
The Scout's Guide to Wild Edibles

"With more than five decades of experience teaching wild edibles to youth, there is no person better qualified than Mike Krebill to write this book. **The Scout's Guide to Wild Edibles** *is a thoughtful selection of some of the best and most common wild plants and mushrooms – with fantastic photography, accurate and concise instructions, and simple, well-tested recipes. Perfect for beginning foragers of all ages."*

~ SAM THAYER, author of *Nature's Garden* and *The Forager's Harvest*

"This is a great book to introduce Scouts or anyone else to foraging. It covers some of the most common, widespread edible plants and mushrooms in a clear, concise manner, with photos that are as instructive as the text. I wish I had this one back when I began to learn foraging myself!"

~ "WILDMAN" STEVE BRILL, author of *The Wild Vegan Cookbook*

"Scouts and outdoor enthusiasts will find this well-thought-out guide indispensable as they search for the tastiest of wild edibles in their local fields and woods. **The Scout's Guide** *is a must-read for the new and experienced forager alike."*

~ J.T. DABBS, III, Scout Executive, Greater Alabama Council; _____ of Southeastern Edibles

The
Scout's
Guide to Wild Edibles

The
SCOUT'S
Guide to Wild Edibles

learn how to forage, prepare & eat 40 wild foods

Mike Krebill

PITTSBURGH

The Scout's Guide to Wild Edibles
Learn How to Forage, Prepare & Eat 40 Wild Foods

Copyright © 2016 by Mike Krebill

ISBN-13: 978-1-943366-06-4

Library of Congress Control Number: 2016938556
CIP information available upon request

First Edition, 2016

St. Lynn's Press . POB 18680 . Pittsburgh, PA 15236
412.466-0790 . www.stlynnspress.com

Book Design – Holly Rosborough • Editor – Catherine Dees
Technical Editor – Melissa Sokulski • Editorial Intern – Morgan Stout

Paper background on cover and divider pages: stockvault.net
Photo credits are listed on page 182.

Disclaimer

The author and publisher expressly disclaim any responsibility for any adverse effects occurring as a result of the suggestions or information in this book. The information is based on the author's personal thoughts and experience, and is not intended to be the final word on identifying and consuming the plants and mushrooms described in these pages. Nor should the information be a substitute for the medical advice of a licensed, trained physician or health professional. If an adverse effect should occur upon contact with any of the plants or mushrooms described in this book, seek medical attention immediately.

Printed in China
on certified FSC paper

This title and all of St. Lynn's Press books may be purchased for educational, business or sales promotional use.
For information please write:
Special Markets Department . St. Lynn's Press
POB 18680 . Pittsburgh, PA 15236

10 9 8 7 6 5

Dedication

This guide is dedicated to Edelene Wood, of Parkersburg, West Virginia. She was the driving force in establishing West Virginia's Nature Wonder Weekend in the 1960s. It has drawn people from all over North America. Held at North Bend State Park on the third weekend of September, it has run continuously ever since then under the sponsorship of the West Virginia Division of Natural Resources. It is an enjoyable opportunity to learn from others and gain experience finding, processing, and feasting on wild foods. Edelene also lent a hand in helping create the North Carolina Wild Foods Weekend, an annual event that began over 40 years ago. Both inspired Sam Thayer to start the Midwest Wild Harvest Festival in Wisconsin in 2005. Edelene has served as president of the National Wild Foods Association ever since it was formed in 1976 to carry on the work of Euell Gibbons. The National Wild Foods Hall of Fame was created to recognize outstanding wild food educators. Through her efforts with the National Wild Foods Association, Edelene has influenced the lives of people in each of the fifty states as well as several foreign countries. Her enthusiasm is contagious.

Edelene Wood

Edelene Wood has devoted her life to promoting wild foods. She has seen them go from survival fare during hard times to highly prized cuisine offered in the finest restaurants. The bandana around her neck is to honor her friend, wild food author and legend Euell Gibbons, who did much to popularize foraging.

TABLE OF CONTENTS

Keokuk 7th graders crack & taste hickory nuts.

INTRODUCTION

I imagine some of you may be wondering about the title of this book and whether the book will be of interest to more than only Boy Scouts and Girl Scouts and their respective leaders. The quick answer to that question is yes. The Scout's Guide is for everyone, from kids to adults to youth group leaders, teachers and parents. Whether you are just a beginner when it comes to edible wild plants and mushrooms, or a seasoned veteran who is looking for new insights and processing tips, the information in these pages will be useful to you.

This is a field guide small enough to deserve the name. It should be easy to carry with you on your outdoor adventures. True, a bigger book might contain more wild edibles. However, I find myself agreeing with wild foods legend Euell Gibbons. In his famous 1962 book, *Stalking the Wild Asparagus*, he wrote "There are many wild plants reported in the literature to be edible that I don't like at all."

With that in mind, I have selected 33 of the better-tasting edible wild plants and 7 of my favorite mushrooms, most of them widely distributed in the U.S. and in Canada's lower provinces. To make the foraging experience even more memorable, I have included 10 engaging activities for individuals or groups and 17 mouthwatering, prize-winning recipes that are kid tested and kid approved.

A fairy ring of Chlorophyllum molybdites *mushrooms, the mushrooms that are responsible for more poisonings in the U.S. than all of the* Amanitas *together.*

Identifying

Accurate identification is paramount. Dr. Peter Gail, a lifelong forager whose Ph.D. is in Plant Ecology, strongly believes that there is a best way to do this: it is to have the plant pointed out to you in the habitat where it grows. Ideally, the person who points it out to you should be a knowledgeable forager with a botany background and years of experience with edible wild plants. This foraging instructor should not only know what the plant is, but should be able to point out how to distinguish it from plants that look similar.

For more than a decade, Dr. Gail strived to develop a directory of foraging instructors across the U.S. His ambitious goal was to find enough people so that there would be someone within 50 miles of anyone wanting help. Eventually, Dr. Gail agreed to pass the task on to Sunny Savage. She worked on it for several years and then found that Deane Jordan (aka "Green Deane") was willing to post the list on his website. To learn if there is an instructor near you, go to http://www.eattheweeds.com and click on "Foraging Instructors."

Harvesting

To have a good experience with edible wild plants and wild mushrooms, it helps to know more than just their identity. You must also know what part of the plant or mushroom is edible. For example, the ripe fruit of a mayapple is a treat and makes a magnificent marmalade, but the rest of the plant is poisonous. While the cap of the scotch bonnet mushroom is delicious cooked, the stem is too fibrous to eat.

Timing the harvest is also critical: Siberian elm samaras (small, flat "wings" with a seed inside) are delicious when the winged portion is green – handfuls of them can be stripped off the tree and eaten on the spot. They are moist and nutty. When the winged portion turns brown, however, they become dry and papery. The length of time they are at their peak is only one week. You can find out when that occurs by making frequent observations beginning before the tree leafs out in the spring.

Preparing

Knowing how to prepare your wild plant helps you get the most from your experience. Acorns offer an excellent example: Most acorns have an abundant supply of tannin that must be leached out to render the acorn meal useful for breads and not unpleasantly bitter. After all, the best part of a successful forage is the enjoyment of eating what you have found!

The Scout's Guide is packed with insights and recommendations gleaned from a lifetime of foraging and my 50-plus years as a wild food educator. May you find this book to be exactly what I intended it to be: a useful field guide to the great adventure of foraging.

Mike Krebill

Plants

In this section, you will find my chosen 33 edible wild plants, their characteristics and uses. Information will be under the following headings:

Range

Habitat

Positive ID checklist

The edible parts of the plant and how to prepare them

A caution note when there's an important observation to share, or a warning about a similar-looking but toxic plant

When to harvest each plant and how to do so sustainably

How to preserve your harvest

Most of the plants found in this guide are widely distributed in the U.S. and in Canada's lower provinces. For convenience in looking up information, they are alphabetized by their common name.

Amaranth, Green

❖ *Amaranthus retroflexus*

RANGE:
Introduced and widespread throughout the United States and Canada

HABITAT:
Wherever soil is tilled or disturbed and moisture is adequate, green amaranth will be among the first and most persistent of weeds.

POSITIVE ID:
- Green amaranth's smooth-edged, oval leaves seem soft, hairy and flaccid. A flaccid leaf is one that appears slightly wilted, like it needs water.
- Also known as "redroot," its taproot usually has a pink or reddish color to it.
- Seedheads at the top of the plant and in several of the leaf axils beneath it have several fingerlike clusters, or spikes, containing hundreds of seeds hidden inside.

At the preferred size for harvesting the leaves for cooked greens, this green amaranth was one of dozens that grew as weeds in community garden plots in Ann Arbor, MI. Note the distinctive red root, helpful in identification, and why the plant is also known as "redroot."

- The ripe seeds are tiny and black, and have a flattened circular disc shape.
- There are no thorns on this plant.

EDIBLE PARTS & PREPARATION:

The young leaves are edible raw or cooked. The seeds are an ingredient in wild food trail bites (award-winning recipe on page 162). Snip off several of the greenish brown seedheads into a paper grocery sack. Roll the sack tightly closed and shake it to free the seeds. As some of the seed coverings will be mixed in, it will be necessary to winnow the tiny black seeds to remove the chaff.

When the plant grows larger, the seedhead begins to develop. The leaves become coarser and more fibrous. The stalk becomes tough and woody as the plant gets taller and taller. This is a stage not worth harvesting.

WHEN TO HARVEST:

Early summer for greens; late summer to early fall for seeds

SUSTAINABLE HARVESTING:

Collecting young leaves and dozens of seedheads will have little impact on this prolific plant.

PRESERVING THE HARVEST:

Drop leaves in boiling water for three minutes, then plunge into ice water. Drain and freeze. Use within 11 months. Keep hulled seeds frozen for up to one year.

The mature plant has an enormous seedhead with finger-like branches and thousands of tiny, shiny black seeds. These seeds can be collected when the seedheads begin turning brown.

Asparagus
❖ *Asparagus officinalis*

RANGE:
A garden and farm escapee in the lower 48 states and Canada's southern provinces that became "wild" thanks to birds eating its berries and pooping the seeds

HABITAT:
Near farm gardens or fields where asparagus was raised. Wild asparagus bushes may be spotted as you drive along a road. Watch for them on the road bank below overhead wires and along fence lines where birds perch.

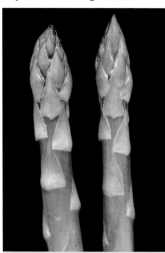

POSITIVE ID:
- Young shoots (spears) are identical to the asparagus spears you might add to your grocery cart in a store. They have triangular, papery bud covers where branches will emerge.
- The open, airy bush that develops from the spear has a woody central stem with thin, wiry branches. Being green, the stem, its branches and the fine, needle-like leaves can capture the energy of sunlight.
- The bush turns golden yellow in autumn.
- The female bush produces 1/4" diameter round red berries which are toxic.

Wild asparagus shoots at their prime. Note that they are unbranched, and resemble asparagus that would be sold in stores. Wild asparagus and garden asparagus are one and the same, differing only in the location where they grow.

EDIBLE PARTS & PREPARATION:

The unbranched spear is the only edible part. For maximum flavor, eat it the same day you collect it. On a camping trip, our Scouts discovered wild asparagus. We dropped the spears in rapidly boiling, salted water for three minutes and ate them immediately. They were bright green, crunchy, and absolutely delicious.

Once the spear begins branching out like this, it becomes too fibrous to eat. It also becomes more and more TOXIC, so do not collect it if it resembles this photo.

WHEN TO HARVEST:

Spring

SUSTAINABLE HARVESTING:

Leave several spears from a group of asparagus plants, to capture the energy of sunlight and keep the roots alive.

PRESERVING THE HARVEST:

Drop spears in boiling water for three minutes, then plunge into ice water. Drain and freeze. Use within 10 months.

Eventually the branches develop into a bush with fine needle-like leaves. Each asparagus stalk visible in this photo represents one bush. Bushes can be either male or female. Female bushes will have hard red berries with seeds inside. These berries are poisonous to people.

Autumn Olive

❖ *Elaeagnus umbellata*

RANGE:
Introduced, invasive and widespread through Central and Eastern U.S., Washington, Oregon, Montana, and the province of Ontario

HABITAT:
Woodland edges, abandoned fields, roadbanks, pastures, orchards and recreational lands

POSITIVE ID:
- This is a multi-trunked woody shrub with occasional thorns.
- Leaves are simple, elliptic, smooth to wavy-edged; grayish-green on upper surface, silvery beneath. Each leaf has a short, silvery-gray petiole.
- Flowers are yellowish-white, 4-petaled and tubular.
- Fruit is silver speckled, red and juicy when ripe.

EDIBLE PARTS & PREPARATION:
The flesh of fully ripe autumn olive drupes is tart, but not astringent. The kitchen tool of choice for separating the pulp and juice from the seeds, skins and stemlets is a food strainer. Dehydrating the juicy pulp produces delightfully sour fruit leather. See page 108 for how

Notice how perfectly plump and round the drupes have become. That's a tip-off that they are probably ripe and ready to harvest. A taste test will soon tell. They should taste tart, and leave no lingering astringency in the mouth.

to make Fabulous Fruit Leather. The juice is a thirst-quenching replacement for lemonade that will wow your taste buds. The fragrant flowers make a nice tea.

WHEN TO HARVEST:
September and October. Ripe drupes that become rose-colored and almost spherical seem promising, but must be taste-tested before picking. Ideally, they should be pleasantly sour with no astringent (mouth-drying) aftertaste. If one drupe tastes good, all the drupes on that particular bush will be worth picking. Otherwise, skip that bush and try another.

SUSTAINABLE HARVESTING:
As long as you avoid breaking a branch, gathering fruit does no harm to the bushes.

PRESERVING THE HARVEST:
Fruit leather can be stored for a year at room temperature in a lidded container kept in the dark.

When the wind blows, autumn olive bushes look silvery gray from a distance.

Black Raspberry

❖ *Rubus occidentalis*

RANGE:
Coast to coast, with over 600 *Rubus* species; especially prolific in the Pacific Northwest. Besides tasty black raspberries, they include bushy blackberries, colorful raspberries, and the trailing, vine-like dewberries.

HABITAT:
At edges of woodland, fields and clearings, along paths, near logging roads, at the base of road cuts

POSITIVE ID:
- Black raspberry is a thorny bush with light green, round canes that arc towards the ground where the tips may root.
- New light green canes often have a whitish, waxy coating that can be rubbed off easily.
- Last year's canes are reddish to purplish brown, lack the white, waxy bloom, and typically branch.
- The leaves are compound with 3–5 toothed leaflets per leaf. (The undersides of the leaflets are light green to almost silvery).
- The fruit is a compound drupe. When fully ripe, the black raspberry is purplish black to black and soft to the touch. When picked, it comes away cleanly from the receptacle on which it grew, leaving a thimble-like hollow. That helps distinguish it from blackberry, which retains its receptacle at the core.

EDIBLE PART & PREPARATION:
Devour handfuls of the raw, ripe berry, or use them to top ice cream, or make syrup by simmering a cup of them with sugar and a little water.

WHEN TO HARVEST:
Typically early summer, depending on location and elevation. After picking, give remaining, unripe berries 7–10 days more to ripen, then return to pick the bushes again.

Two nice fruit clusters of black raspberries ripe for the picking. Rose Barlow once told me that she had picked 32 gallons of wild black raspberries in a single year. She explained that she had found eight nice patches. By the time she finished picking the eighth one, enough berries had ripened to return to patch number one and repeat the process.

SUSTAINABLE HARVESTING:

As long as you don't destroy the bushes, picking the fruit should cause no harm.

PRESERVING THE HARVEST:

Freeze the berries on a cookie sheet, then pour them into a quart bag. Vacuum seal the bag and stick it back in the freezer.

Most young black raspberry canes have a bluish-white waxy bloom that can be rubbed off.

Black Walnut
❖ *Juglans nigra*

RANGE:
Native to 35 states
and southern
Manitoba, Ontario
and Quebec

HABITAT:
Rich bottomland soils
of stream valleys

POSITIVE ID:
- The black walnut
  tree has alternate,
  pinnately-
  compound leaves
  1–2' long with
  15–23 leaflets.
- Yellow-green,
  1-1/2–3" round
  fruit consists of a
  nut encased by a
  fleshy husk.
- When broken open
  and exposed to air,
  the husk flesh color
  changes from a
  yellowish white to dark brown.
- The brown nut has a corrugated surface.

Close-up of a black walnut tree showing a cluster of its tennis ball-like fruit (walnuts) and the long compound leaves. A leaf can be up to 24" long and may have from 15 to 23 leaflets. The terminal or end leaflet is often missing. Because walnuts may be high in the tree, foragers typically wait until they drop to the ground in October to collect them.

EDIBLE PARTS & PREPARATION:
Put on dishwashing gloves or equivalent to avoid staining your hands. Step on the green husk with a boot and twist your foot to pop the nut loose. Pull off clinging husk pieces, then rinse and brush or power wash the walnuts. Dry indoors on a tarp in front of a fan for two days. Let ripen and dry for two more weeks

(no fan). Crack with a vise or hammer and use a nutpick to remove large pieces of the edible nutmeat. The strong flavor of black walnuts is perfect in brownies and ice cream (see Cinnamon Black Walnut Ice Cream recipe, page 137).

WHEN TO HARVEST:
October

SUSTAINABLE HARVESTING:
Collecting walnuts from the ground does not harm trees.

PRESERVING THE HARVEST:
Huskless, unshelled black walnuts may be stored at room temperature for two years. Extracted nutmeats are high in fats and oils that can turn rancid at room temperature, so they are best kept frozen. If vacuum-sealed first, they will last in the freezer for three years.

Left: walnut with tennis-ball like husk. Right: walnut with husk removed, then power washed. The brown nutshell has a corrugated surface.

Blueberry & Huckleberry

✤ Vaccinium spp.

RANGE:
Widespread throughout the United States and Canada

HABITAT:
Many habitats, from wetlands to mountaintops. Best in sunny locations.

POSITIVE ID:
- Bush grows from 1–8' tall with 1-1/2–3" long, alternate, elliptical leaves.
- The pendant, bell-shaped flowers are white and fragrant.
- Berries are powder blue to blue or black when ripe, except for the red huckleberry, whose berries are red to orange.
- Five-pointed star-shaped pattern is on the bottom of the berry, a remnant of the blossom.
- Berries typically grow in clusters.
- Ripe berries are juicy, with a pleasantly sweet, mildly tart flavor.

Knee to waist-high blueberry bushes were a welcome sight as my sister Lynn and I hiked in the mountains of North Carolina. A handful of blueberries provided a thirst-quenching treat and an energy boost.

EDIBLE PARTS & PREPARATION:

The berries are edible raw and make a delicious, energy-filled and thirst-quenching nibble – a wonderful trail treat when hiking. Dried leaves make a decent tea. The flowers, if you should be lucky enough to be present when blooming, are a floral taste treat. See page 144 for the Double-Good Blueberry Pie recipe.

WHEN TO HARVEST:

Spring for flowers; mid to late summer for berries. Leaves throughout the season

SUSTAINABLE HARVESTING:

Don't damage the bushes when picking. Leave some berries for birds and other animals. Birds will help spread the patch.

PRESERVING THE HARVEST:

Freeze a single layer of berries on a baking sheet, then pour them into a freezing container with a screw-top lid. Label with a date and use within a year for the best flavor. Berries can also be dehydrated. I've not tried drying and saving the leaves, but if you do, I'd suggest using them within a year so that the flavor isn't lost.

On a family camping trip in the Mt. Hood River Valley east of Portland, Liz – my Oregon sister – introduced me to mountain huckleberries. These grew on bushes from five to seven feet tall.

Burdock, Common

❖ Arctium minus

RANGE:
Widespread and invasive in the U.S.
(except Texas and Florida), and the southern
provinces of Canada

HABITAT:
Barnyards, pastures, open woods, sunny patches along
trails

POSITIVE ID:
- Burdock is a weed with large rhubarb-like leaves. The underside of the leaf is covered with a thin, woolly mat of fine white hairs. Leaf petioles may be reddish to purplish at the base.

- Although considered a biennial, burdock's flowering stalk may take four or more years to appear, according to a study at Michigan State University. It depends on environmental conditions and how much energy the root has been able to store for the event. The stalk can range from 4–7' tall.

- Thistle-like flowers give way to the round, infamous burdock burs.

- Each bur is a stick-tight whose tiny hooked ends catch in clothing and dog fur.

Burdock leaf rosette in early May.

EDIBLE PARTS & PREPARATION:

My favorite way to eat burdock is to peel the tender, non-woody sections of the taproot, cut up into matchstick-sized pieces and do a stir-fry with carrots. This is a Japanese side dish known as kinpira gobo. Gobo is Japanese for burdock. The company-pleasing recipe is on page 132.

WHEN TO HARVEST:

While the taproot from burdock that hasn't yet sent up a flowering stalk can be dug at any time, it will be at its largest in the fall and at its sweetest in early spring.

SUSTAINABLE HARVESTING:

Taking the taproot kills this often despised weed. If you wish to grow more in your own garden, use the seeds found inside a dried bur.

Burdock's burs are seedpods that hitchhike on mammals to new locations. When the mammal tries to scratch or rub them off, the burs break apart, releasing the seeds. The burs are difficult to remove from dog fur, and vexing when stuck in a sweater. Pull on a piece and the rest remains behind. It seems to take forever to remove it all.

PRESERVING THE HARVEST:

Burdock roots can be kept cool in barely damp soil, and retrieved for use during the winter. If you have a chance to shop at an Asian market in a large city, you may be able to buy refrigerated packages of gobo.

Cattail

❖ *Typha* spp.

RANGE:
Widespread in U.S. and
Canada

HABITAT:
Wet soil; shallow, still or
slowly moving water

POSITIVE ID:

- Cattail is an emergent
  aquatic plant 4–9' tall.
  Up to 6 long, narrow
  leaves 1/4–3/4"
  wide surround an
  unbranched, cylindrical
  stalk.

- In late spring, the yellow
  pollen-producing male
  flower spike tops the
  stalk. The larger female
  flower spike is below it.

- The female spike
  resembles a brown
  hotdog as tiny seeds
  mature in late summer.

- Rhizomes – finger-thick
  starch storage organs –
  run horizontally through
  muck or sand, often connecting plants.

*Common cattail's hotdog-like seedhead
begins ripening to its brown color in
July. Filamentous green algae covers the
surface of the pond behind the cattail.
Neither the blanket moss, as the algae is
often called, nor cattails will be found in
fast moving streams.*

EDIBLE PARTS & PREPARATION:
Separate the young shoot from its base by grasping the leaves
together and steadily pulling upwards. The white tip/core is edible
raw. Roast rhizomes at the edge of a fire; split open to chew the

hot, white, fibrous inner core. After extracting the starchy essence, spit out the wad of fibers. Husk male flower spikes and treat them like corn on the cob. Boil them, butter them, sprinkle a little salt on them, and nibble away. Stir the pollen into pancake batter for yellow, high-protein pancakes. Sharply pointed white lateral buds at the end of rhizomes make a fine cooked vegetable. The brown hotdog part of the cattail provides perfect texture as a vegetarian substitute in a mock barbecued pulled-pork recipe, page 134.

Instructor Sunny Savage points out the edible parts of the cattail she and her class harvested at a Wild Food Summit in mid-June. The starch-filled rhizome goes from her left forefinger to over her shoulder. The Summit, held for 10 years on tribal land in northern Minnesota, provided an opportunity to gain many insights on wild foods. Participants witnessed the reverence that Native Americans have for Mother Earth. Sustainable harvesting of wild foods is a way of life for them as it should be for all people. The Summit was hosted by the White Earth Tribal and Community College Extension Service.

WHEN TO HARVEST:
Late spring for "cattail corn" and pollen from male flower spikes; spring and summer for shoots; late August through fall for cattail head; year-round for rhizomes and laterals. (Rhizomes should be a mottled tan and white, with a white starchy core. If gray or black, they are too far-gone. Laterals should be firm and white. If gray or black or squishy, don't collect them.)

SUSTAINABLE HARVESTING:
Leave part of the colony to regenerate.

Chokecherry
❖ *Prunus virginiana*

RANGE:
Widespread throughout the U.S. (except in the southeastern tip), southern Canada and the Northwest Territories

HABITAT:
Few plants have as wide a range of habitats as chokecherry. It can be found in a variety of evergreen and deciduous forest types, and in deserts, basins, plateaus, savannas, flood plains and prairies.

POSITIVE ID:
- Chokecherry is a thicket-forming shrub or small tree.
- The small cherry-like fruit is borne in racemes and has an astringent taste until slightly past the fully-ripe stage (see When to Harvest). Fruit color ranges from red to purple or black.
- Each fruit is 1/4 – 3/8" in diameter. Like other cherries, it is a drupe, with a single seed covered by a hard shell.
- Leaves range from 1– 4" long, are finely toothed and are broadly elliptical to ovate (egg-shaped).
- The bark has raised horizontal rows of lenticels.

EDIBLE PARTS & PREPARATION:
Fully ripe chokecherries make a fabulous fruit leather, juice, jelly and syrup. Hop over to page 108 for how to make Fabulous Fruit Leather.

WHEN TO HARVEST:
Late August, depending on the plant and location. Harvest when the fruit is fully ripe to slightly wrinkled, with color ranging from crimson red to a dark reddish-purple to black. They yield to pressure and are juicy, and should roll off the pedicels and into your hand when touched. If they still cling tightly, give them another week or two to ripen before trying again.

Bitterness can vary from tree to tree, so it helps to do a taste test before putting them in the pail. Ripe chokecherries' inherent bitterness is less pronounced when they are a bit overripe and the skin is slightly wrinkled. Cooking the fruit will also help dispel some of the bitterness.

SUSTAINABLE HARVESTING:
Picking the fruit does no harm to the plant.

PRESERVING THE HARVEST:
Pit the cherries and can, dry, or freeze the juice and pulp. Make fruit leather, jam, jelly or syrup.

The bitterness of chokecherries varies from tree to tree and is lessened when they are a bit overripe and slightly wrinkled.

Dandelion
Taraxacum officinale

RANGE:
Widespread throughout the U.S. and Canada

HABITAT:
Lawns

POSITIVE ID:
- Dandelion is a common yellow-flowering plant, abundant in the spring.
- Its deeply notched, toothed leaves stay in a basal rosette.
- Several flowers grow from a single rosette. Each flower has its own leafless, unbranched stalk. The flower head is 1–2" in diameter.
- Flower stalks are hollow. When broken, the stalk bleeds a bitter white latex, as does the midvein of each leaf and the taproot.
- The seedhead is spherical. Seeds are attached to a pad in the center. Each has a thin stem tipped by a feathery umbrella-rib-like pappus, which functions as an open parachute to carry the seed away.

EDIBLE PARTS & PREPARATION:
The whole plant is edible. Wild foods expert Sam Thayer enjoys snacking on raw flower stalks, but I find them too bitter. Rapidly growing leaves are the least bitter; gather them from the shaded edge of mowed areas, where they turn vertical to compete for sunlight with the deep grass around them. Remove the bitter tasting midvein. Taproots can be roasted and ground to use in coffee or ice cream. Making dandelion flower donuts (page 138) is an easy and fun activity loved by thousands of students and Scouts. For something more savory, try making Dandy Burgers (page 141). To prepare dandelion flowers for cooking, see page 121.

WHEN TO HARVEST:
Spring for the leaves, flower buds and flowers; late summer, fall and early spring for the taproot

SUSTAINABLE HARVESTING:
Dandelion is such a persistent lawn weed that the only way you might not have a plentiful supply to harvest in the future is to use an herbicide to kill it and other weeds. If you want to have dandelions forever, don't use herbicides.

PRESERVING THE HARVEST:
Leaves can be blanched and frozen. Roots can be baked to dehydrate them. Squeezed flowers (see Preparing Dandelions, page 121) can be frozen. Use before the next spring.

Dandelions grow rapidly when competing for sunlight. The unbranched, leafless hollow stem leading up to the flower head distinguishes them from plants that look similar.

Japanese Knotweed
❖ *Polygonum cuspidatum*

RANGE:
Invasive and widespread since introduced for landscaping. Currently in much of North America except for the southwestern U.S., Louisiana and Florida, and the provinces of Manitoba and Saskatchewan in Canada.

HABITAT:
Roadsides, streambanks, and disturbed ground; preferably moist sites

POSITIVE ID:
- Japanese knotweed is an erect, multi-stemmed, non-woody plant that grows from 3–10" tall.
- The stems are jointed, hollow and resemble bamboo.
- Its leaves are smooth-edged and would appear heart-shaped if they weren't flat at the base near the petiole.
- Small, greenish white flowers are clustered in showy spikes.

EDIBLE PARTS & PREPARATION:
Cut off young, still-flexible shoots up to 15" tall. Immerse the cut ends of shoots in a bucket about 1/3 full of water to keep them from wilting. At home, remove

Japanese knotweed along a Michigan fence line in September, showing stalks, leaves and flowers. This dense stand was 9–10' tall.

and discard leaves. To reduce fibrousness, slice stems crosswise into thin coins. For longer, less flexible shoots, peel them before slicing as you might peel celery. Boil until soft, then strain. It will be remarkably similar in taste to stewed rhubarb: sour and slightly bitter. Sweeten to taste and serve, use in a mock rhubarb pie, or dehydrate and turn into fruit leather.

Japanese knotweed shoots harvested from a West Virginia roadbank on the third week of April.

WHEN TO HARVEST:
Early to mid spring. Harvest at the shoot stage when few leaves have unfurled.

SUSTAINABLE HARVESTING:
This is one of the world's most aggressive invasive plants. Cutting shoots seems to have no impact on it at all. However, while you don't need to be concerned about sustainable harvesting,

Japanese knotweed seed clusters

you should respect the wishes of the property owner, who may have planted them there for landscaping purposes.

PRESERVING THE HARVEST:
Perhaps the best way to preserve Japanese knotweed is to turn it into fruit leather. See page 108 for how to make Fabulous Fruit Leather.

Lambsquarters
❖ *Chenopodium album*

RANGE:
Widespread throughout the U.S. and Canada

HABITAT:
Gardens and disturbed soil

POSITIVE ID:

- Lambsquarters is a common bare-soil weed with a distinctive grayish-green appearance towards the center of the growing tips. On magnification, the color comes from tiny beads of whitish wax. These feel like fine cornmeal to the touch, and can be rubbed off.

The distinctive grayish-green new growth of lambsquarters helps one identify it at a glance. The leaf's triangular shape resembles a leg of lamb, which is also known as a quarter, hence "lamb's quarters" or "lambsquarters." Another common name is goosefoot, due to the shape of the leaf.

- Triangular to diamond-shaped leaves alternate up the stem. The stem begins to branch when about a foot tall and can become a bush up to 7' tall, but typically ranges from 3–5' tall.

- Reddish streaks may appear on the ridged stem, and there's a spot of reddish purple in every leaf or stem axil.

- Tiny black seeds are produced in multiple spikes of clustered, rubbery, green, small round cases that turn yellow in September when the seeds are ready to harvest.

EDIBLE PARTS & PREPARATION:

Young plants 4–8" tall can be cooked stems and all. In taller, older plants, stems become too woody, so collect the tender terminal or axillary clusters of leaves and use them as a potherb. The plant mass reduces greatly when cooked. It can be used as a spinach substitute. Lambsquarters may be steamed, boiled, stir fried, incorporated into a quiche or added to a cheese omelet. Some people eat the tender young leaves raw in salads, although I don't care for them that way.

Although it might be easier to notice that the stem is ridged on an older lambsquarters plant where it is more sharply defined and streaked with red or purple, another characteristic is visible here: there's a spot of reddish purple in the leaf axils.

The seeds are edible and can be used to add nutrition to Wild Food Trail Bites, a prize-winning recipe on page 162.

WHEN TO HARVEST:

Leaves and stems: Spring. Seeds: September. When winnowing seeds, watch out for tiny caterpillars.

SUSTAINABLE HARVESTING:

Lambsquarters will self-sow if it's allowed to set seed.

PRESERVING THE HARVEST:

The leaves can be preserved by drying, pressure canning, or blanching and freezing.

Mayapple
❖ Podophyllum peltatum

RANGE:
Eastern 2/3 of U.S. except for the Dakotas; found in Ontario and Quebec

HABITAT:
Deciduous woodland floors with patches of sunlight

POSITIVE ID:
- Umbrella-like leaves are the hallmark of this 1–2' - tall woodland perennial. Each plant has one or two of them. Two leaves are necessary for the plant to flower and produce fruit.

Ripe mayapples – some have small rotten spots that I cut out before using them to make marmalade.

- A single white flower grows from the Y-shaped crotch of the stem. Up to 3" in diameter, with 6–9 waxy petals, it has a smell like the tropical taste of the ripe fruit.
- The single fruit is a berry having the shape and size of a hen's egg.
- Ripe fruit color ranges from creamy white to yellowish white to lemon yellow.

CAUTION:
The green, unripe fruit is toxic, as are the seeds, leaves, roots and rhizome. Be very careful and avoid all fruit that has even a hint of green.

EDIBLE PARTS & PREPARATION:
The fully ripe berry is the only edible part of this otherwise toxic plant. It can be eaten raw or used in a beverage, cake, or ice cream, but my favorite way to enjoy it is to make the Mayapple Marmalade recipe on page 150.

WHEN TO HARVEST:
Mid-summer: mid-July to mid-August. Collect berries when fully ripe (light yellow to lemon yellow with no hint of green). Ripe berries feel slightly soft.

SUSTAINABLE HARVESTING:
Collecting the fruit does not harm the plant.

PRESERVING THE HARVEST:
Process mayapples within a day of harvesting them. Wash the fruit, cut off the blossom and stem ends, and quarter the fruit. Bring it to a boil in a pot with a cup of water, then lower the heat to a simmer. Cover and cook for 15 minutes, stirring occasionally to be sure it doesn't burn. Strain through a food mill. Keep the juice and pulp, and discard the skin and seeds. Vacuum seal and freeze the juice and pulp. Use within six months.

Two mayapple plants with ripe fruit in late July. The fruit is shaped like a hen's egg, and ranges in size from a small egg to a large egg, with a medium size most commonly found.

Milkweed, Common
❖ *Asclepias syriaca*

RANGE:
Eastern 2/3 of U.S. except Florida; western states: in Montana and Oregon only; present in Saskatchewan, Manitoba, Ontario and Quebec

HABITAT:
Fields, roadsides, fencerows, meadows, prairies

POSITIVE ID:
- Milkweed is a non-woody perennial with broad, rubbery, elliptical leaves along a stem typically 3–5' tall. The stem does not branch until it reaches the flower clusters.

- Smooth-edged leaves bleed white latex when torn, as does the rest of the plant. The leaf underside has short, woolly hairs.

- Clusters of flower buds and flowers are spherical and 3–4" in diameter. The flowers are crown-shaped and sweet smelling.

These milkweed pods are too big to use. They would be tough and fibrous.

- The seedpods are about 4" long, light green at first. The surface is covered with rows of soft, rubbery hair-like projections. The pods contain small, circular brown papery seeds and white silken threads. When pods ripen and split open, the threads form parachutes for seed dispersal.

EDIBLE PARTS & PREPARATION:

Young shoots up to 8" high are tasty boiled, buttered and salted. Steam flower buds like broccoli. Small seedpods under 2" long are tasty cooked, although given the rubbery hair-like projections, the mouth feel is strange.

WHEN TO HARVEST:

Shoots: early spring
Flower buds and flowers: late spring to early summer
Pods: early summer

SUSTAINABLE HARVESTING:

Harvest only a few shoots per collecting site; rotate sites when collecting shoots to give plants an opportunity to recover. This is one of the milkweeds that provide food for monarch butterflies. Harvest only where the milkweed is plentiful, and take only what you need for a single meal.

Common milkweed shoots have pubescent (hairy) stems, and the underside of the leaves is also pubescent. This is one of many ways they can be distinguished from the hairless common dogbane, which has a skinnier shoot and tastes bitter when cooked.

PRESERVING THE HARVEST:

Blanch, vacuum seal, and freeze shoots and flower buds. Pickle young seedpods that are less than 2" long.

Mulberry
❖ *Morus* spp.

RANGE:
U.S., British Columbia, Ontario and Quebec

HABITAT:
Thrives along moist woodland edges and streams, in floodplains and pastures, and along fencerows. It is commonly seen in cities, often along property lines.

POSITIVE ID:
- Each mulberry fruit is made up of a columnar-shaped collection of small, fleshy drupes tightly attached to a green stem that runs through it. This type of fruit is called an aggregate or collective fruit, not a berry. A typical sized fruit ranges from 3/8–1/2" in diameter by 1" long.
- Fruit color is variable, and consequently, mulberry names can seem confusing. Ripe red mulberries *(Morus rubra)* range from a dark, deep red to black. White mulberries *(Morus alba)* can have white, lavender, or blackish purple fruit. Black mulberries *(Morus nigra)* are a welcome exception, as they are black.
- White and red mulberries ripen in late spring, while black mulberries ripen in summer to late summer. A tree's mulberries don't ripen all at once, but over an extended period of 4–6 weeks, which is good news for foragers who like them.
- The outer bark of a young mulberry tree typically has a yellow to orange tint to it. The young bark of an older tree as seen through fissures of its older, outer bark may be yellow; the heartwood is greenish-yellow to orange; the root bark is orange.
- Every mulberry leaf is simple as opposed to compound, and serrated instead of smooth edged. The leaves may be lobed or unlobed, and one often sees a variety of lobed shapes on a single tree. The leaves can be very glossy.

EDIBLE PARTS & PREPARATION:

Eat ripe fruit raw, make it into ice cream, bake it in a cobbler, or turn it into taffy. Juice the mulberries to make a drink. Here's a simple how-to link for making a drink: www.phamfatale.com/id_1724/title_Mulberry-Juice/

Making mulberry taffy with family or friends is a memorable activity. (See recipe, page 153.)

Only one ripe fruit here, the dark one. Unripe fruit can cause gastrointestinal problems, so leave the red ones to ripen longer. Generally speaking, ripe fruit will feel soft and juicy, and will stain your hands when picked.

WHEN TO HARVEST:

Late spring to early summer, depending on location. (In parts of Florida, mulberries ripen in February.)

SUSTAINABLE HARVESTING:

Picking (or shaking) ripe mulberries from the tree doesn't harm the tree.

PRESERVING THE HARVEST:

Spread mulberries apart on a baking sheet and individually freeze. Once frozen, double bag and gently squeeze the air out or vacuum seal and return to the freezer. Use before the next season rolls around. Extract the juice by forcing mulberries through a kitchen strainer with a pestle (rounded stick) from a mortar and pestle; by wearing dishwashing gloves and squeezing through cheesecloth; by using a food strainer; or by steam extraction with a juice extractor (I use a Mehu-Liisa extractor) – then refrigerate or can. Mulberries may also be dried.

Oak
❖ *Quercus* spp.

RANGE:
Lower 48 states except for Idaho; southern provinces of Canada

HABITAT:
Upland woods

POSITIVE ID:
- The oak tree produces acorns as its fruit.
- Acorns have a cap with a twig attachment and a thin-shelled nut below, which completely encloses an easily extracted nutmeat.
- Oak trees have alternate branching

White oak acorns on the ground in Iowa, late September.

EDIBLE PARTS & PREPARATION:
Acorns are edible, but very bitter due to the tannins they contain. I want to give credit to "Jan," a member of rec.food.recipes newsgroup, for the simplest and fastest method I've come across yet for removing tannins (described at http://trishgood1.tripod. com/otwild.html#Acorn%20Pound). Shell out the nutmeats and grind a cup of them in a blender full of water. Pour into a dishtowel-lined colander in the sink. Run cold water over the acorn meal and stir to leach out the bitter-tasting, water-soluble tannins for at least 8 minutes. Turn off the water and taste a pinch. If bitter, repeat the process until the bitterness disappears. (See page 130 for an award-winning recipe.)

WHEN TO HARVEST:
Fall: collect from ground from mid-September through mid-October

SUSTAINABLE HARVESTING:
Gathering dropped acorns from below an oak doesn't harm the tree.

PRESERVING THE HARVEST:
Press 2 cups of damp, processed acorn meal flat inside a quart-sized vacuum-seal freezer bag. Vacuum-seal it, then freeze it. It will keep up to 4 years. The flattened package takes up little space in the freezer and thaws rapidly in a bowl of warm water when you want to use it. Most recipes require 2 cups or less. If it is less, you can easily reseal and refreeze the leftover meal. Damp meal works fine if added with the wet ingredients. In fact, bread loaves made with damp meal are lighter and more flavorful than ones made with dry meal.

Perfect white oak acorns on a tree in Michigan in early September.

Oxeye Daisy
❖ *Leucanthemum vulgare*

RANGE:
Widespread. Introduced in all 50 states. Present throughout every Canadian province except Nunavut.

HABITAT:
Frequently planted in flower gardens and along roadbanks as an ornamental wildflower species. May show up in nearby hayfields and pastures.

POSITIVE ID:
- In their first year, the plants consist of a dark green clump of shiny leaves just a few inches high. The leaves are lobed and shaped like miniature white oak leaves.
- The second year plants develop flowering stalks that are typically 18–24" tall.
- The white petaled flowers, which are 2–2-1/2" in diameter, have yellow centers.

Oxeye daisy flowers on a roadbank.

EDIBLE PARTS & PREPARATION:
The first-year leaves are edible raw and can be used as a trail nibble or as a salad or sandwich ingredient. They have a sweet, carroty taste.

WHEN TO HARVEST:
Spring

SUSTAINABLE HARVESTING:
Always leave some of the clump's leaves behind to capture the energy of sunlight, feed the plant, and regenerate new leaves. The best practice for sustainability is to collect leaves sparingly from several clumps instead of decimating one or two.

PRESERVING THE HARVEST:
There are several edible wild plants that I prefer to enjoy only at the peak of the season in which they are at their freshest, most tender and flavorful. This is one of those plants. I take only what I need for a nibble, a sandwich or a salad, using what I've gathered right away. Enjoy snacking, but don't try to preserve this harvest.

Young daisy plant with a rosette of leaves; the leaves will increase in number and become a dark, glossy green with time.

Pawpaw
✥ *Asimina triloba*

RANGE:
Native to 29 states in the East, South and Midwest. Planted elsewhere for edible landscaping. Grown in orchards from Virginia and North Carolina to California, Oregon and Washington. Also found in Canada: southern Ontario.

HABITAT:
Prefers rich alluvial soils of stream valleys and adjacent woods

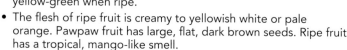

POSITIVE ID:
- Pawpaw leaves are up to 1' long by 5" wide and are smooth-edged. They're shaped like magnolia leaves, but are softer, thinner and more flexible.
- The crushed leaves smell like used motor oil.
- The fruit is kidney shaped, 2–6" long and 1–3" wide. It may grow in clusters. The skin is pear green and may lighten to yellow-green when ripe.
- The flesh of ripe fruit is creamy to yellowish white or pale orange. Pawpaw fruit has large, flat, dark brown seeds. Ripe fruit has a tropical, mango-like smell.

EDIBLE PART & PREPARATION:
Cut the fruit in half crosswise. Slowly squeeze the pulp and seeds out of the skin and into a French-fry basket. Dispose of the skin. Remove seeds by gently pressing the pulp through the basket and into a bowl. Use immediately, put it into a zip bag to exclude air, or vacuum seal and freeze. The more the pulp is exposed to air, the bitterer it becomes. Edible raw, papaw pulp is a perfect substitute for bananas in banana bread and makes stellar ice cream.

Tom Wahl directs attention to one of the biggest pawpaws on his u-pick Red Fern Farm near Wapello, Iowa. A ripe pawpaw will yield to a gentle squeeze, meaning that it is ready to pick.

WHEN TO HARVEST:
Fall: Pawpaws ripen from mid-September to mid-October. A ripe pawpaw yields to a gentle squeeze.

SUSTAINABLE HARVESTING:
Collect only ripe fruit and process it the same day; never pick every fruit on a tree. Start your own pawpaw orchard with the seeds.

CAUTION:
Allergic reactions are possible in sensitive individuals.

PRESERVING THE HARVEST:
Kathy Dice, who with her husband Tom Dahl owns a pawpaw orchard in Iowa, recommends double-bagging as a preferred method for excluding air. (See details on page 176.)

Persimmon, Common

❖ *Diospyros virginiana*

RANGE:
Native to 30 states, from California to the Atlantic Coast.
Larger, seedless persimmons from Korea, China and Japan are
commercially grown in California, Louisiana and Florida.

HABITAT:
Prefers sandy, well-drained soils and the rich soils of river
bottomlands in the South.

POSITIVE ID:
- A tree with small, round orange fruit. The fruit ranges from
  3/4–2-1/4" in diameter, and is typically smaller than a golf ball.

- The fruit hangs on the tree after the leaves fall, making the tree easy to identify.

- The bark has an unusual blocky pattern, somewhat like an alligator's skin.

- The fruit is astringent until fully ripe. When ripe, it often drops to the ground. A ripe persimmon is soft and flexible.

The fruit hangs on the tree after the leaves drop.

EDIBLE PARTS & PREPARATION:
Fresh or fully dried leaves make a respectable tea. Roasted seeds
have been used as a coffee substitute since Civil War times. The
fully ripe fruit is delicious raw, cooked or dried. It can be used in
bread, cookies, ice cream and pudding. Judging ripeness is an
important skill. If ripe, it will be on the ground or easily shaken

from the tree; it feels soft and looks wrinkled; the dry, dark brown calyx will twist off easily; it should taste sweet, not bitter or puckery. Check out Fiona McAllister's tips on collecting and processing at http://persimmonpudding.com/harvest/pulp-laundrybag.html.

A fully ripe persimmon is soft and flexible. The dark brown calyx on top will twist off with little effort.

WHEN TO HARVEST:

Fall: Harvest persimmons that drop on the ground in September and October.

SUSTAINABLE HARVESTING:

Get permission from property owners to collect persimmons that fall on the ground. This does no harm to trees, making it a sustainable approach, and property owners will appreciate your picking up the fruit, which can make a sticky mess underfoot in a yard.

PRESERVING THE HARVEST:

I vacuum-seal and freeze the persimmon pulp in heavy-duty plastic freezer bags. I just taste-tested a package that is three years old. Still good.

The blocky bark on a persimmon trunk is distinctive.

Plantain
❖ Plantago major, Plantago rugelii

RANGE:
Widely distributed throughout the U.S. and Canada

HABITAT:
Compacted ground, such as school playgrounds, the edges of gravel driveways, and dirt paths. Almost as common as dandelion in yards and school lawns and along sidewalks where herbicides are not used.

POSITIVE ID:
- Plantain leaves are spoon shaped with prominent parallel veins on the underside.
- When the leaf stalk is slightly torn and slowly pulled apart, celery-like strings may be seen.
- The seed stalk is a slender, unbranched spike.

Rugel's Plantain in July with its distinctive seed spikes.

EDIBLE PART & PREPARATION:
The spring leaves, before the flowering spike appears, make tolerable leaf chips. With scissors, snip off the widening base of every leaf blade where the petiole joins it, and discard to reduce

the bitterness. Wash the leaves, blot dry and place in a medium-sized bowl. Add 1 tablespoon extra virgin olive oil. Work the leaves around with your hands to lightly coat with oil, then place leaves on a baking sheet. Roast at 350° F for 10-15 minutes until crispy like potato chips. Sprinkle with a little salt. The small, young, yellowish-green leaves from the center of the plant are slightly bitter but can be used raw in salads.

The pronounced rib-like, parallel veins on the underside of spoon-shaped leaves help distinguish plantain from other common lawn weeds. The leaf on the left belongs to Common Broadleaf Plantain, Plantago major. To its right is Rugel's Plantain, Plantago rugelii. The tip of its petiole ranges from red to purple. Sometimes the color is as long as the one shown. Sometimes only the very end is reddish-purple.

WHEN TO HARVEST:
The leaves are least bitter in the spring, before the flowering spikes start growing.

SUSTAINABLE HARVESTING:
Collect only a few leaves from each plant so more of the leaves may grow back.

PRESERVING THE HARVEST:
While one might blanch and freeze the leaves or dry them, this is another plant that I prefer not to save from one year to the next. I simply gather them fresh when I want to eat them. Plantain is fairy common in lawns and once you are familiar with it, you will see it often.

Pokeweed

Phytolacca americana

RANGE:
Native to 40 of the lower 48 states in the U.S. Absent from Idaho, Montana, North Dakota, South Dakota, Wyoming, Nevada, Utah and Colorado. Found in Ontario and Quebec.

HABITAT:
Disturbed soils, vacant lots, organic farms, edges of fields and woods

POSITIVE ID:
- Pokeweed's oval leaves are 8–12" long by 2–5" wide and are smooth-edged and hairless
- The plant's hollow, branching stalk is often tinged with reddish-purple.
- Fruit clusters are in racemes that droop downwards; their dark purple berries borne on short, magenta colored pedicels.

EDIBLE PART & PREPARATION:
Edible parts: the above-ground young shoot, up to 6" tall; and leaves with no red or magenta color in the veins or leaf stalk. Boil for at least 10 minutes in 2–3 changes of water to remove and break down toxins. Try this recipe from Mike Rasnake: Spread cream cheese over a wonton/egg roll wrapper. Place a cooked shoot at one edge, fold over the sides, roll it up and seal with egg wash. When ready, deep-fry a few at a time in hot oil at 375° F until light golden brown, about 45 seconds. Drain on paper towels.

One of the best places to find a pokeweed shoot in spring is at the base of last year's dead, hollow pokeweed stalk.

Side branch of pokeweed shows the smooth-edged leaves and the drooping racemes of purple berries. Notice the magenta pink pedicels.

CAUTION

Incompletely leached and undercooked pokeweed can cause explosive diarrhea. (An unforgettable personal experience!) The root, seeds and reddish-purple parts of the plant are poisonous. The dark purple berries are considered toxic by some; others have made pies from them in which the berries were cooked.

WHEN TO HARVEST:

Spring

SUSTAINABLE HARVESTING:

Collect only one shoot per plant yearly to allow the plant to produce a replacement that can develop leaves to make food.

PRESERVING THE HARVEST:

The processed shoots or leaves may be canned.

Purslane
❖ *Portulaca oleracea*

RANGE:
Introduced or native to all states in the U.S. (except Alaska), and Canada's southern provinces

HABITAT:
Disturbed soils of gardens and flowerbeds

POSITIVE ID:
- Purslane is prostrate, forming a mat on the ground.
- The leaves are paddle shaped and succulent-like
- The stems are round, rubbery and as thick as a pencil; reddish on top and greenish underneath.
- NO milky juice bleeds out when a leaf is torn.

EDIBLE PART & PREPARATION:
The tender tips of stems, including leaves, may be eaten raw in salads, baked in a quiche or added to a stir-fry. Flexible stems up to the thickness of a pencil may be pickled. Check out the quick and easy microwave purslane pickle recipe on page 148.

Purslane leaves are thick like a succulent.

CAUTION:
Eat small amounts, as purslane contains calcium oxalates. A large intake of oxalates for several days in a row may damage excretory organs like the kidneys, but occasional small amounts should cause no problem for a healthy person.

Purslane growing as a weed in a friend's garden.

WHEN TO HARVEST:
Mid to late summer

SUSTAINABLE HARVESTING:
Use a pair of scissors to harvest portions of a plant so that the remainder can continue to grow and produce seeds.

PRESERVING THE HARVEST:
I don't recommend trying to freeze, can or dry purslane. It is fleshy, succulent and mucilaginous, making it difficult to dry. Freezing and thawing breaks down the cell structure, as does canning. This results in an unpleasant sliminess. Pickling works, but purslane is one of the plants I prefer to wait and enjoy when the season arrives again.

Serviceberry
❖ *Amelanchier* spp.

RANGE:
Various species present throughout the U.S. (except Hawaii) and Canada

HABITAT:
Woodlands; does best in the open or at the edges of woods where sunlight is plentiful

POSITIVE ID:
- Serviceberry plants are shrubs to small trees with smooth, light gray bark; older tree bark may have dark gray vertical grooves.
- The leaves are egg-shaped to elliptical, with finely-toothed edges.
- Round clusters of white flowers appear in the spring before trees leaf out, brightening the edge of woods.
- Individual flowers are 1" long, fragrant, and have 5 narrow white petals spread apart in a star shape.
- The berries, 3/8–1/2" in diameter, are in small clusters. They resemble blueberries and have a 5-pointed crown on the bottom of each berry. The fruit becomes red and finally purple as it ripens. Each berry contains a few vanilla-flavored seeds.

Picking serviceberries for breakfast on a canoe trip.

The dark purple berries are the ripest.

EDIBLE PART & PREPARATION:
The ripe fruit is edible raw, but the berries of some Amelanchier species taste better than others. No preparation is necessary. The berries can be used any way that you might use blueberries.

WHEN TO HARVEST:
Summer: Ripe berries, which are dark purple and soft, are typically found from mid-June until mid-August. Not all of a bush's berries ripen at the same time, so you may return and pick more.

SUSTAINABLE HARVESTING:
Picking berries does no harm to the bush or tree as long as branches aren't broken.

PRESERVING THE HARVEST:
Serviceberries can be dried, frozen or canned.

Shagbark Hickory
❖ *Carya ovata*

RANGE:
North Dakota, south to Texas and east to
Atlantic Coast, except for South Dakota and
Florida; found in Ontario and Quebec in Canada

HABITAT:
Common associate of oak trees in upland oak-hickory forests

POSITIVE ID:

- Older tree trunks have gray to grayish brown strips of bark from 6" to 2 or more feet long. The strips often curl away from the tree, being attached in the middle and loose at one or both ends.

- Compound leaves are 10–18" long, each with 5 serrated leaflets. The terminal leaflet is the largest, and those to the side of it are larger than those close to the leafstalk.

- A 4-parted, 1/2"-thick husk covers the ridged hickory nut. It may split open before or after the nut drops in the fall.

- The nutmeat resembles a short pecan, and has a sweet and pleasant taste.

The shaggy bark of shagbark hickory makes identification a snap.

EDIBLE PARTS & PREPARATION:
Collect and crack the hickory nuts. (For a technique that can yield large pieces of nutmeats, check out Cracking & Shelling Hickory Nuts, starting on page 105.) Carefully examine extracted nutmeats

Each shagbark hickory nut is enclosed in a 1/2"- thick, four-parted husk. The husk is thicker than other hickory nuts and breaks apart more readily, often on impact when it drops from the tree and hits the ground.

to remove any shell shards left from cracking. The hard, sharp shell fragments can get wedged between teeth or into a person's gums when enjoying cake, cookies or other treats. The shaggy strips of bark can be used to give a hickory-smoked flavor and a maple syrup color to sugar syrup. Recipe is on page 158.

WHEN TO HARVEST:
Pick up hickory nuts when they drop in September and October.

SUSTAINABLE HARVESTING:
Collecting hickory nuts does no harm to the tree.

PRESERVING THE HARVEST:
Hickory nuts left in the shell will keep for two years if air-dried and protected from rodents. Once they are cracked and shelled out, however, nutmeat oils can turn rancid, so it is best to vacuum seal and freeze them.

Sheep Sorrel
❖ Rumex acetosella

RANGE:
Widespread throughout the U.S. and most of Canada's provinces

HABITAT:
Often found in disturbed soil, grasslands, and along roadbanks; does well in acidic, sandy soils

POSITIVE ID:

- Sheep sorrel is a weed whose new season growth begins as a cluster of leaves – some spoon-shaped, some arrowhead-shaped or resembling a fish on a stick.

A nice bunch of sheep sorrel leaves before the flowering stalk emerges. At this stage they are tender and pleasantly sour.

- The wiry, branching, 4–18" tall flower stalk has small reddish and greenish-yellow flowers above a few alternate, small leaves that clasp the stalk; from a distance, a large patch of them gives a reddish yellow-green tint to that location.

- Before the flowering stalk emerges, the tender new leaves have a pleasantly sour taste

EDIBLE PART & PREPARATION:
The tender new leaves are edible raw, and impart a lemony taste to sandwiches, soups and quiche.

CAUTION:
Eat only moderate amounts, as sheep sorrel (like purslane and yellow wood sorrel) contains calcium oxalates. Large amounts of oxalates, eaten often, may be hard on a person who has a history of kidney stones. Small amounts should cause no trouble for a healthy person.

WHEN TO HARVEST:
Spring to early summer. Harvest before the flowering stalk emerges. The young leaves will be soft, juicy, and flavorful.

SUSTAINABLE HARVESTING:
With the fingers of one hand reaching over the top, squeeze a cluster of leaf blades together. Clip the leaf blades off their stalks with a pair of scissors. New leaves will emerge from the base after this mowing as the plant recovers.

Sheep sorrel plant with seedhead.

PRESERVING THE HARVEST:
Sorrel is one of several plants that I don't go to the trouble to preserve from one season to the next. If you wanted to try, my suggestion would be to rinse the leaves and drop them into boiling water, blanching them for two minutes. Then, pour them through a strainer and dump them into a bowl of ice water. Afterwards, pat them dry between two towels. Double-bag in a zip bag and freeze. Use them in a potato-sorrel soup within three months.

Siberian Elm
❖ Ulmus pumila

RANGE:
Widespread and invasive in U.S. and
Canada

HABITAT:
Fencerows of farms; property borders in
towns

POSITIVE ID:
- Siberian elm is a weedy tree that sheds twigs
  and branches, littering yards.
- The leaves are 1-1/2 – 2" long, alternate,
  serrated, and pinnately veined.
- Buds are reddish brown, rounded and sparsely
  hairy.
- Clusters of dime-sized, wafer-like samaras appear
  to surround twigs in the spring. (Chinese elm,
  a similar-looking tree, produces its samaras in
  the fall.)
- When backlit, a single small lentil-shaped, light
  brown seed can be seen inside each round samara.

EDIBLE PARTS & PREPARATION:
Strip off a small handful of the yellow-green samaras, pop them
into your mouth and chew. The seed inside is slightly nutty, and
the samara is pleasant to taste.

WHEN TO HARVEST:
Mid to late spring: There is a one-week window of opportunity to
gather these when they are at their prime, making them the most
time-sensitive of all the edible wild plants I have ever enjoyed.
At that time, the leaves have yet to appear, and the samaras
are a uniform bright yellow-green, soft and flexible like lettuce.

Once their color begins to fade and they dry out, they are not as pleasant to chew. The green stage will vary depending on your location. In southeastern Iowa, where I live, that week occurs around tax time, April 15.

SUSTAINABLE HARVESTING:
Stripping off a handful or two of seeds does not damage the tree.

PRESERVING THE HARVEST:
Best eaten fresh. I refrigerated a handful of seeds for a week, and froze a small bag for a month. They were picked at their prime. Not bad, but not nearly as good as when freshly picked.

A soft, moist cluster of Siberian elm samaras at the perfect stage after a spring rain. Thanks to Sam Thayer for writing about Siberian elm in The Forager's Harvest. *This is one of my favorite nibbles.*

Silver Maple
❖ *Acer saccharinum*

RANGE:
Across the U.S., except for Oregon and 7 western states from Montana to New Mexico; found in Saskatchewan, Ontario and Quebec

HABITAT:
Floodplains and urban lawns

POSITIVE ID:
- Silver maple is named for the silvery underside of its leaves.
- It has opposite branching: each twig, branch, and leaf has another straight across from it.
- Leaves have five major lobes. Veins branch out into these lobes. The two lobes nearest the petiole are the smallest, the two below them at the widest point of the leaf are large; the bottom lobe forming the tip of the leaf is at least as large if not larger. Deeply indented serrations occur along the lobes of the leaf.
- A single maple seed is found in the swollen part of the key (see Glossary), its seed case fused to the samara – a papery, winged structure that spins like a helicopter to carry the seed on a windy day. Tens of thousands of keys hang in pairs or singly and spin to the ground each spring.

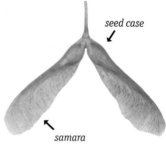

seed case

samara

Paired silver maple keys

Silver maple branches with leaves; note the silvery underside of the leaves

EDIBLE PARTS & PREPARATION:
Toss a bowlful of green keys with a spoonful of vegetable oil (peanut adds a nice flavor if no one is allergic), and toast them on a baking sheet at 375° F for 20 minutes or until lightly browned. Sprinkle with salt. (See page 127 for more about processing and preparing silver maple keys.)

WHEN TO HARVEST:
Spring: Harvest when the samaras range in color from green to brown, but still hang in the trees.

SUSTAINABLE HARVESTING:
Picking samaras does not harm trees.

PRESERVING THE HARVEST:
Don't bother. Gather fresh the next spring.

Stinging Nettle
❖ *Urtica dioica*

RANGE:
Native to Europe, widespread throughout the U.S. (though not reported in Arkansas) and Canada

HABITAT:
Common in sunny openings of swamps and floodplain woodlands, near streams, in moist rich soil, along fences and in roadside ditches

POSITIVE ID:
- The plant has coarsely-toothed, heart-shaped to long, narrow leaves opposite one another along a stem typically 4–8' tall.
- The veins appear sunken into the leaf when viewed from above, and on the leaf surface when viewed from below.
- On the upper part of the stem, branching, string-like clusters of green flowers emerge from where leaves join the stalk.
- Transparent stinging hairs are found on the stem, the leaf stalks, along the main vein on the underside of the upper leaves and on the flower clusters.

Older stinging nettle becomes very fibrous. Use tips and leaves only.

EDIBLE PARTS & PREPARATION:

Nettles are nutritious – the greens are high in protein, vitamin C, vitamin A, calcium, magnesium and iron. Young plants up to a foot high can be collected and steamed or boiled for a spinach-like side dish. (When harvesting the plant, I wear gloves to avoid getting stung; some foragers don't.) Cooking destroys the stinging property and makes the plant safe to consume. As the plant grows older and tougher, leaves can be picked and used fresh or dried for tea.

WHEN TO HARVEST:

Young plants: early spring. Leaves may be collected throughout the growing season.

SUSTAINABLE HARVESTING:

Nettle is a perennial plant that can recover so long as some of the shoots are left.

PRESERVING THE HARVEST:

Nettle can be blanched and frozen. It can also be canned or dried.

Young stinging nettle plants

Sumac
❖ *Rhus glabra, Rhus typhina (R. hirta), Rhus copallinum*

RANGE:
R. glabra: widespread throughout the lower 48 states of the U.S. and the southern provinces of Canada; *R. typhina:* most common in northeastern states; *R. copallinum:* most abundant in southeastern states

HABITAT:
Roadbanks, fence and power lines, and the edges of woods

POSITIVE ID:

- Shrubs occur in clonal groups from underground runners.
- Groups may be female with red fruit clusters or male without fruit clusters.
- Long, pinnately compound leaflets turn scarlet in the fall. Leaflets are serrated in smooth sumac *(R. glabra)* and staghorn sumac *(R. typhina)* and smooth-edged in winged sumac *(R. copallinum).* The winged sumac leaf has a winged mid-rib, which gives it its name.
- The fruit head is a cone-shaped cluster of red drupes.

Smooth sumac fruit

  It is upright, like a red Christmas tree in *R. glabra* and *R. typhina,* and leaning over in *R. copallinum*
- *R. typhina* drupes are covered with short hairs, and the young twigs are velvety. The twigs resemble the antlers of a male deer in velvet, hence the common name of staghorn sumac.

EDIBLE PART & PREPARATION:

The sour covering of the drupes makes pink lemonade when it flavors water. Concentrated, it serves as a wild substitute for lemon juice. Check out the researched technique for making consistently good sumac lemonade, on page 123; and two excellent recipes on page 160.

WHEN TO HARVEST:

Summer: The sumac fruit clusters are at their prime from mid to late summer, when they taste super-sour. They will appear uniformly bright red, like those of Smooth Sumac, pictured.

SUSTAINABLE HARVESTING:

Leave some fruit heads for seed dispersal by birds.

PRESERVING THE HARVEST:

Vacuum seal drupes in a heavy-duty freezer bag. Store in a freezer for up to 4 years.

Staghorn sumac shrubs

Sunroot

❖ *Helianthus tuberosus* (aka Jerusalem Artichoke)

RANGE:
All states except Alaska, Hawaii, Nevada, Arizona and New Mexico. Most abundant from the Dakotas south to Kansas, eastward through the Midwest to Massachusetts and south to Virginia. In Canada from Saskatchewan eastward to Nova Scotia.

HABITAT:
Grasslands, field and woodland edges, fencelines and roadbanks

POSITIVE ID:

Sunroot flower

- Sunroot is a small-flowered sunflower, with a flower head 2–4" in diameter. It has 10–20 thin yellow petals (ray flowers), typically 1/2" wide and a yellow to yellowish-orange disk in the center that is 1/2–3/4" in diameter. Flowers August to October.

- The stalk is 4–9' tall, unbranched until near the top. It feels sandpapery to the touch due to its short, stiff hairs. The raspiness and lack of branching until the top help identify it in late autumn or early spring when it is time to dig the tubers.

- The leaves are opposite on the lower stalk and alternate on upper branches.

- Stiff hairs on the top of the leaf point towards the tip and resist a finger slid backwards

- Leaves feel sandpapery to the touch and have three prominent veins and a winged petiole.

EDIBLE PART & PREPARATION:
Peel and enjoy tubers cooked in a crockpot stew or soup, where they impart a wonderful smoky potato taste.

CAUTION:
The tuber contains inulin. In sensitive individuals, gas, bloating and pain can occur when bacteria in the large intestine break inulin down. Anyone with irritable bowel syndrome might wish to avoid the consequence of eating these tubers.

WHEN TO HARVEST:
Fall and spring: Dig in late fall or early winter before the ground freezes, or else in very early spring. Doing so gives the indigestible starch inulin a chance to break down to fructose, so the tubers are less likely to cause flatulence.

SUSTAINABLE HARVESTING:
Leave a few plants so the patch can regenerate.

PRESERVING THE HARVEST:
Pickle the tubers.

Clusters of sunroot flowers provide beautiful color

Wild Grape
❖ *Vitis riparia* and other species

RANGE:
Dozens of species found throughout the lower 48 states and in eastern lower provinces of Canada. *Vitis riparia* (Riverbank Grape) has the widest native distribution.

HABITAT:
On bushes and trees along streambanks and woodland edges; a common fence climber wherever fences exist

POSITIVE ID:
- A wild grape vine may sprawl over the ground or use tendrils to climb fences, bushes and trees in its quest for sunlight.
- The leaves are toothed and maple leaf shaped.
- Older vines are covered with shaggy strips of bark.
- The fruit looks like miniature clusters of pea-sized, bluish-purple Concord grapes.
- Each grape has 2–3 round seeds with a short, pointed end.

Wild grapes

EDIBLE PART & PREPARATION:

Y-shaped tendrils of vines provide a thirst-quenching nibble on a hot day. Large leaves can be preserved in brine and used to make dolmas or dolmades (stuffed grape leaves). Ripe grapes may be eaten raw, turned into juice or made into wild grape jelly. Making and enjoying wild grape popsicles is a memorable group activity. To prepare a small batch for your family, try Jessica Garrett's recipe on page 164.

Wild grape leaves and tendrils are very distinctive.

WHEN TO HARVEST:

Late summer through mid-fall

SUSTAINABLE HARVESTING:

Use a pair of scissors to clip off clusters of ripe grapes; this will not harm the vine.

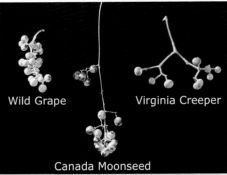

Wild Grape

Virginia Creeper

Canada Moonseed

CAUTION: *Similar-berried, but toxic Canada Moonseed and throat-irritating Virginia Creeper may grow next to Wild Grape. Distinguish them by the differences in their berry clusters.*

PRESERVING THE HARVEST:

Can the juice, freeze and use popsicles within a couple of months, or make wild grape jelly, which will last for several years (if you have enough willpower).

Wild Plum

❖ *Prunus americana* and other species

RANGE:
Lower 48 states and lower provinces of Canada

HABITAT:
Woodland openings and edges, pastures, fencerows and thickets,
abandoned fields

POSITIVE ID:

Wild plums

- Wild plums grow on woody shrubs or small trees, which occasionally have thorns and spur shoots.
- The bark has raised horizontal lines called lenticels; twigs have raised corky dots, also known as lenticels.
- The leaves are egg-shaped, 1-1/2 – 4" long. They alternate along the stem and have finely toothed edges and a long, pointed tip.
- Wild plum flowers appear before the leaves in early spring. They are fragrant and white to pinkish. Each one has 5 petals and about 20 long stamens that protrude from the middle of the flower.
- The 1" plums are round and yellow to red or purple when ripe. Each has one pit, enclosing the single seed.

EDIBLE PART & PREPARATION:

The ripe fruit is edible raw. The skin is tough and sour so you may wish to remove the pit, then put the plums through a food mill to separate the pulp from the skins. The pulp can be used in a variety of ways, but wild plum jam is my favorite.

WHEN TO HARVEST:

Mid-August to mid-September. A ripe plum may fall into your hand when touched. It should yield to a gentle squeeze. A taste test proves whether the plum is ripe or still astringent.

SUSTAINABLE HARVESTING:

Picking wild plums doesn't harm the tree.

PRESERVING THE HARVEST:

Plums can be canned, dried, pickled or turned into fruit leather or jam. The pulp and juice may be canned as a base for a delightful ice cream.

Wild plums in Colorado.

Yellow Wood Sorrel

❖ *Oxalis stricta* and other yellow-flowered
  Oxalis species

RANGE:
Absent from Alaska and Hawaii, but introduced or native to all
other U.S. states and Canada's southern provinces

HABITAT:
Disturbed soils of
gardens and flower
beds, in lawns, along
paths, around trees;
will grow in sun but
is more often seen
where shade exists

*Sorrel leaves resemble clover, but each leaflet is
heart shaped.*

POSITIVE ID:

- This non-
  woody plant is
  distinguished from
  clover by having
  5 yellow petals
  per flower, 3 heart-shaped leaflets per leaf, and upright, ridged
  seedpods.
- To avoid stress in dry weather the leaves may fold down like a
  closed umbrella.
- The leaves and seedpods have a sour, lemony taste.
- Yellow wood sorrel is a small plant, typically less than a foot tall.

EDIBLE PART & PREPARATION:
Leaves and seedpods may be eaten raw, added to a salad or
sandwich, or used in a soup or quiche. They turn an unappetizing
greenish-brown shade when heated. While the stems are edible
(and may not be objectionable if they are young and tender and
used in a salad or sandwich), their texture isn't as pleasant a nibble
as the leaves and seedpods.

CAUTION:

Eat small amounts, as yellow wood sorrel contains calcium oxalates. Large amounts of oxalates, eaten frequently, might damage excretory organs in sensitive people. Small amounts, eaten a few times a year, should cause no problem for a healthy person.

WHEN TO HARVEST:

Spring through late summer

SUSTAINABLE HARVESTING:

Use a pair of scissors to "mow" the plant's top so that the remainder can continue to grow and produce seeds.

PRESERVING THE HARVEST:

Preserving yellow wood sorrel is not worth the effort. Simply collect it seasonally.

Yellow wood sorrel

Wild Mushrooms

In this section, I have chosen 7 mushrooms that I like to eat. An essential part of positive mushroom identification is making sure that **ALL** (not some) of the characteristics of the mushroom match those listed in your reference book. Let's say that you found a photo of a mushroom that looks like your unknown. You start checking the detailed description. Your mushroom has 11 of the 12 characteristics stated, but it has brown spores instead of the white ones mentioned in your book. That means one thing for sure: you haven't figured out what you've got yet, and you can't make a safe positive ID. It's best to walk away. Better safe than sorry!

Once you have confirmed the identity of an edible mushroom and are absolutely confident that you know what it is, heed this prudent precaution if you are eating it for the very first time: leave some of the mushroom uncooked and labeled in the refrigerator in case you might have incorrectly identified it or in case you turn out to be allergic to it. Phone a friend and ask your friend to call you back an hour or so after you have eaten the mushroom to make sure you are all right. Tell your buddy where the mushroom is if a 911 call is needed. Eat only a small part of the cooked mushroom. Wait long enough to know how your body reacts to it before you consider eating more a day or two later. One more thing: **ALWAYS** cook mushrooms. Many people have gotten sick from eating raw morels.

Frontiersman Davy Crockett's motto is a really good one to remember, whether you are dealing with wild mushrooms or edible wild plants: "Always be sure you are right, then go ahead."

Chanterelle
❖ *Cantharellus cibarius*

RANGE:
Throughout North America

HABITAT:
On the ground under oaks or conifers

POSITIVE ID (all must be true):
- Chanterelles resemble the photo on the right. The entire mushroom is pale egg-yolk yellow to apricot-colored.

Young chanterelles with solid stipes, washed and ready to sauté.

- The stipe is solid, fairly sturdy and has no ring. Unless it's been roughly hollowed out by maggots, the flesh inside stipe and cap is white.
- There are flattened, blunt ridges under the cap instead of thin, sharp-edged gills. The ridges, connected by a network of veins, fork near the edge of the cap and taper down the stipe.
- The cap of the young mushroom is flat topped, dry and not sticky. It has a rolled skirt margin with wavy edges.
- Chanterelles grow on the ground, not on wood; singly or in pairs, but never in big clusters.
- They may have a fruity odor like apricots, or no odor at all.
- Older chanterelles are funnel-shaped and irregular.
- The flesh doesn't change color when it's bruised.

SEASON:
Early summer through fall

Chanterelles take on a great variety of shapes as they grow. This is the shape of young chanterelles at the stage I consider prime for collecting.

CAUTION:

Two poisonous lookalikes – The poisonous pumpkin-colored Jack O'Lantern *(Omphalotus illudens)*, grows in large clusters on stumps or buried wood. It has crowded, sharp-edged gills under the cap. The gills don't fork. It may smell unpleasant. Avoid the poisonous False Chanterelle *(Hygrophoropsis aurantiaca)*, too, which has true gills that fork repeatedly, and is soft and flimsy compared to the firmness of a chanterelle.

COLLECTING TIP:

When picking, cut the stem with a knife to keep the mushroom clean. Inspect for maggot tunnels; crumble and discard the mushroom if you find them.

CULINARY RATING:

10/10. This is one of the most sought-after and prized mushrooms in the world.

The holes in this chanterelle's stipe mean that the mushroom is infested with maggots.

PRESERVING THE HARVEST:

Dry and powder, or sauté slowly and freeze.

Giant Puffball
❖ *Calvatia gigantea*

RANGE:
Throughout North
America; West
Coast has *Calvatia
booniana*

HABITAT:
On soil in lawns,
pastures, and
meadows; just
inside woodlands

Giant puffballs in October

POSITIVE ID (all must be true):
- The giant puffball mushroom resembles those in the photo.
  The entire mushroom is white and round, and ranges in size
  from that of a softball to that of a volleyball, soccer ball, or
  basketball. It may seem somewhat flattened, like a big lump
  of dough.
- Short, dark, root-like structures anchor the puffball to the
  ground.
- When sliced in half from top to bottom, the mushroom shows
  no outline of a stipe or gills.
- The flesh inside is all white like the inside of a marshmallow.

SEASON:
Summer/Fall

CAUTION:
If the interior of the puffball is turning yellow, green, or yellowish
brown in places and smells bad, it is too far-gone to use. White
maggots may be inside it, but can be difficult to see unless they
wiggle. Inspect the skin for tiny holes. Also advisable: cut into the
mushroom below the holes.

TWO POISONOUS LOOKALIKES:

(Easily determined by cutting the mushroom in half from top to bottom.) Deadly poisonous *Amanita* mushrooms start out white and round, but reveal a stipe and gills developing inside when cut open. Stinkhorn mushrooms begin developing inside an egg-shaped structure. When cut open it is gelatinous inside.

COLLECTING TIP:

A long-bladed fillet knife with a sheath is a good thing to have in your collecting basket. It can be

Andy Benson's storage dilemma. Sometimes it's better to just collect one!

used to slice from top to bottom of the puffball to be sure of its identification and to check its condition. One large puffball feeds a crowd, so don't bring more home than you can possibly use.

CULINARY RATING:

7/10. See the recipe for puffball pieces on page 155.

PRESERVING THE HARVEST:

Puffballs can be partially cooked for a few minutes, frozen on trays so they hold their shape, then vacuum-sealed and kept frozen. Use before the next season begins. Add them to soups or stews. Can also be sliced into bread-thickness cubes, dried, and ground into flour for making gravy or mushroom-flavored pancakes.

Hen of the Woods
❖ *Grifola frondosa*

RANGE:
Widespread and common east of the Rocky Mountains; more difficult to find west of the Rockies. Commercially grown and marketed as maitake.

HABITAT:
On the ground, very close to the base of an oak tree

POSITIVE ID (all must be true):

Close-up showing the dusty look of the lobes on an older hen. This is caused by fine white spores falling down from the lobes above them.

- *Grifola frondosa* is a polypore, which drops its spores from thousands of tiny holes on the underside of the mushroom.

- The mushroom consists of stacked, clustered rosettes of overlapping fan-shaped lobes, which are attached to a branching stem-like, whitish structure that looks somewhat like the internal stems of cauliflower. The lobes can be tiny when the mushroom is young, but grow up to 2-3" long by season's end.

- The lobes start out whitish, becoming brown to smoky gray on top. They may or may not have white borders. Underneath, the lobes are white and have many tiny pores. White spores fall from the tiny pores beneath each lobe and may land on lobes below, giving a dusty appearance.

- When bruised with a thumb or finger, the white underside of a lobe stays white; it does not darken to brown or black like the black-staining polypore, *Meripilus sumstinei*, (a similar-appearing edible mushroom). Also, when you split the lobe of the black-staining polypore you'll see stringy fibers, whereas they are not present in the hen of the woods.

SEASON:
Fall: Hens are most often spotted in September and October.

COLLECTING TIP:
Carry a sheathed fillet knife in your basket. The long-bladed knife makes it easier to cut the cluster free from its attachment to the ground, and trim away any undesirable portions.

CULINARY RATING:
10/10 when young. Older hens may have an acrid taste. My favorite way to enjoy this mushroom is to charcoal grill it. Pull the lobes off, place them on the grill and baste them with barbecue sauce toward the end of their cooking.

PRESERVING THE HARVEST:
Break or cut the lobes off, slice up the stems, partially cook the pieces, vacuum seal them, then freeze for no longer than a year.

Looking down from above on a very nice hen of the woods. Immediately behind it is the base of an oak tree.

Morel, Common Yellow

⟡ Morchella esculentoides

RANGE:
Most common and widely distributed morel of the 19+ species in North America

HABITAT:
River bottomlands that haven't flooded in the last three years; sparsely wooded slopes; dying and recently dead elm trees; old apple orchards; near oak, ash, black cherry, black locust, and cottonwood trees

Common yellow morel

POSITIVE ID (all must be true):

- Yellow morels resemble the photo and are typically 2–4" tall, but may grow up to 12" tall if conditions are right.
- They have an egg-shaped pitted cap with unaligned ridges. The ridges between the pits are smooth (they look like they have been sanded) when the mushroom is young, and become sharp edged as the mushroom ages. The ridges are tan, not dark brown or black.
- The pitted part of the morel is fully connected to the stipe.
- When sliced in half from top to bottom, the mushroom is hollow.
- The morel produces a white spore deposit when covered with a bowl and left for several hours.

SEASON:
Spring

COLLECTING TIP:
Cut the morel's stem and use a one-inch paintbrush to brush off any dirt before putting it in a collecting basket or mesh bag, (but not in a plastic bag as morels can spoil). Once home, rinse to remove sand, dirt and critters before cooking it.

CAUTION:
Some people are allergic; others become allergic from eating too much, too often. Morels are poisonous raw, and must be cooked.

CULINARY RATING:
10/10.

PRESERVING THE HARVEST:
Slice morels in half lengthwise and thoroughly dry them. Store in glass jars for up to 20 years. For the best "fresh" taste, I recommend following the semi-dry preservation technique researched and refined by McFarland and Mueller, in their book, *Edible Wild Mushrooms of Illinois & Surrounding States.*

One of the key findings from a 10-year study of the distribution and abundance of morels in Iowa was that morels begin to appear when soil temperatures reach 53° F. In the spring, I carry a digital thermometer in the glove compartment of my car.

Oyster Mushroom
❖ *Pleurotus ostreatus*

RANGE:
Throughout North America

HABITAT:
On hardwood, especially living
and dead elm tree trunks,
logs, or stumps; may appear
on soil (but will be attached to
wood or roots underground).
Often commercially available
in stores, either fresh or dried.

POSITIVE ID (All must be true):

Oyster mushrooms in the fall may have brown caps.

- Oyster mushrooms resemble the mushroom pictured in the photos. They smell "fishy," like the ocean beach.
- Spore color ranges from creamy white to pale lilac.
- Mushrooms grow in overlapping clusters. Each individual mushroom has a semicircular shell-shaped cap, hence the name. The size of the cap ranges from 3–12" in diameter. The cap is white to silvery gray from early spring through late summer and may become dark tan to brown in the fall.
- When the mushroom is young, the margin of its cap is rolled under. Also, the thin, white-to-cream-colored gills under the cap are forked near the edge of the cap. These gills run nearly all the way down to where the short, lateral, off-center stem (if there is one) is attached to the wood.

SEASON:
Oyster mushrooms have been found in all seasons of the year, but summer through fall is the prime time to hunt them.

COLLECTING TIP:

Carry a sheathed fillet knife in your collecting basket to carefully cut the clusters away from the bark beneath. Handle the mushrooms gently.

CAUTION:

A poisonous lookalike – the poisonous Angel Wings, *Pleurocybella porrigens*, is smaller, has thin translucent flesh, and lacks a fishy odor.

CULINARY RATING:

8/10. Oyster Mushrooms are popular edibles, although some people are allergic to them.

PRESERVING THE HARVEST:

Slice thin and dry

A photogenic group of oyster mushrooms on a log covered by moss. Note several key characteristics: 1) mushrooms grow in an overlapping cluster; 2) the caps are whitish to silvery gray and the gills below are white to cream-colored; 3) the margins of the younger caps are rolled under; 4) the gills run nearly all the way down the short, lateral, off-center stem toward its point of attachment.

Scotch Bonnet
❖ *Marasmius oreades*

RANGE:
Throughout North America

HABITAT:
On soil in lawns, pastures, parks, cemeteries, practice fields

POSITIVE ID (all must be true):
- Scotch bonnet mushrooms must resemble the photo on the opposite page. They are small and tan, usually less than 3" tall.
- These mushrooms have tan caps 1-1/2 – 2" in diameter, which are often slightly darker in the center, where there may also be a bump. The cap is wavy, with upturned margins that show the gills.
- Widely spaced cream-colored gills beneath the cap are slightly notched before being attached to the stipe, but they do not run down it. Other gills start at the margin but never reach the stipe.
- The mushroom stipe is thin and tough. Splitting it with a thumbnail and pulling it apart will reveal thread-like fibers connecting the pieces.
- The patch of grass where this mushroom grows in groups, in arcs or in a fairy ring will be darker green than the rest of the lawn.
- Spore print is white.

The dark green ring in the grass is a good place to look for the Scotch bonnet mushroom, Marasmius oreades. It may be difficult to spot as the caps are seldom as tall as the grass. The ring is darker green than the surrounding grass, since the mushroom breaks apart minerals and organic matter in the soil, acting as fertilizer.

This is a superb photo of Marasmius oreades, *very typical of their appearance.*

SEASON:
Summer/Fall: August to November

COLLECTING TIP:
Scotch bonnets rarely grow alone, so keep checking the darker green patches of grass. Even if they appear to be dried up, these mushrooms rehydrate nicely.

CAUTION:
Poisonous mushrooms may also grow in groups, arcs or fairy rings, making the grass around them greener. Their size may even be similar, but they differ from Scotch bonnet in the details and in their appearance.

CULINARY RATING:
9/10.

PRESERVING THE HARVEST:
Remove the stem and dehydrate caps. The dried caps rehydrate quickly and add a nice flavor to soups and pasta when cooked.

Sulfur Shelf
✤ *Laetiporus cincinnatus* and *Laetiporus sulphureus*

RANGE:
Throughout North
America

HABITAT:
L.cincinnatus: on
the ground at the
base of oak trees;
L. sulphureus:
always on wood –
the sides of trees,
logs, or stumps of
hardwoods

The yellow-pored sulfur shelf is always found on wood, either on the side of a living or dead tree, on a fallen tree like this one in West Virginia, or on a stump. It has a bright orange top with sulfur-yellow margins and underside. Overlapping shelves, like the ones in this photo, are the norm.

**POSITIVE ID
(all must be true):**
L. cincinnatus, **White-Pored Sulfur Shelf**
- Study the characteristics mentioned in the photo captions.
- Tiny pores may be seen on the underside of the lobes.
- Lobes are soft and flexible (never woody) and don't turn black when bruised with a thumb.

L. sulphureus, **Yellow-Pored Sulfur Shelf**
- Study photo captions.
- The underside of the sulfur shelf has tiny pores.

SEASON:
Both mushrooms may be found in the spring, but are more abundant in the summer and fall.

CAUTION:
Avoid collecting sulfur shelf mushrooms that grow on any of the following types of trees: eucalyptus, locust, hemlock, pine, fir, spruce, larch or tamarack. The reason is that while *Laetiporus*

genus mushrooms occur on those trees, they are different species than the ones in this account, and they have sickened many people.

COLLECTING TIP:
L. cincinnatus – collect the entire mushroom if it looks good.
L. sulphureus – collect only the portions tender enough to be easily cut with a knife.

CULINARY RATING:
10/10 for *L. cincinnatus*; 8/10 for *L. sulphureus*. Cooked, each has the texture of chicken breast meat, making it a fine vegetarian alternative in chicken recipes.

PRESERVING THE HARVEST:
Dry, or sauté and freeze either mushroom.

This white-pored sulfur shelf is found on the ground, usually at the base of an oak tree. In contrast to the yellow-pored sulfur shelf, it has a regular, well-formed shape that consists of a rosette of overlapping lobes. Viewed from above, it resembles an opened rose. The upper surface of each lobe is pale orange to a faint salmon-pink, while the edge of the lobe and its underside are white. The lobes feel velvety smooth on top and they appear slightly wrinkled.

Projects & Activities

This section contains 10 activities that have enlivened Scout meetings and have proven to be enjoyable and instructive sessions for foragers and school classrooms as well. They offer challenges, useful information and wisdom gleaned from experience in doing them. Tested and true, every one of them is a hands-on learning opportunity.

A Backpacking Make-Lunch Challenge

Scouts crave adventure and like to take on a challenge. They want to boldly go where they have never gone before. They get tired of the same old stuff, and bored with inactivity. To have a dynamic unit that attracts and keeps members, imaginative activities are a must.

With these thoughts in mind, I challenged our Patrol Leader Council to incorporate backpacking into our June campout. None of the boys had ever backpacked before, so the novelty was certainly there. No one even owned a backpack, but that wasn't a deterrent. Our troop is an old troop, and our storeroom shelves held over a dozen donated backpacks and individual Scout cook kits.

If you work with a Scout troop or if you are a group leader with a school or church, our experience with this challenge might give you ideas for doing something similar. Spoiler alert: everyone had a wonderful time, learned something they hadn't known before, and came away with a new sense of accomplishment.

THE PROCESS:

What we brought. For our troop, normally heavyweight campers, this wasn't a true backpacking experience, as we did not alter our behavior. Our tents are not backpacking tents, they are heavy 4-person tents primarily designed for use at a weeklong summer camp. We took two butane tanks and a butane stove stand. Our vehicles transported four large plastic totes of cooking, dining and dishwashing equipment, two Dutch ovens, a wok, and two cast iron frying pans. We had three large picnic coolers, lanterns, a dining fly, and two water coolers, a hatchet, an axe, a splitting maul, a 2-lb. sledge hammer for driving tent stakes, a bag of charcoal, a charcoal starter, and a shovel for moving hot coals… not even close to lightweight camping.

Mother Nature and a change of plans. Our intent was to drop the boys off and let them backpack their sleeping bags and clothes to the campsite, about a mile and a half inside the state forest. However, we got a late start, darkness was approaching, and it began raining and kept raining, and raining. Fortunately, we were able to get two large tarps over a couple of picnic tables, high enough to allow our cooks to prepare and cook our meals.

Backpacking. After breakfast dishes were done the next morning, the boys decided to backpack to a lake about a mile away. A couple of lads brought fishing poles, knowing ahead of time that fishing was permitted. Each person's challenge was to come up with and cook his own lunch, finding wild edibles enroute. Soup was a suggestion; boys had brought their water bottles and a cook kit. I carried instant rice that they could add as one ingredient.

Wild onion or field garlic?

Wild soup. On the hike, we found several edible wild plants that the boys added to their soups: wild garlic, yellow wood sorrel and plantain among them. The boys enjoyed the experience and got creative with their soups. Most added rice.

One even dropped a handful of M&Ms in his soup! It may have seemed like a good idea at the time, but it looked and tasted disgusting, and he didn't want to finish it.

Fire. Even more challenging than creating a soup was building the fire to cook it. The rain had thoroughly soaked all the wood overnight. The boys had to carve away the wet outer layers in order to find wood dry enough to create shavings to light. The rain started again and fortunately the pots covered enough of the fire to keep it going.

The results. The boys succeeded against the odds. They backpacked, identified and brought back edible wild plants, made soup, built a fire and fed themselves. An unforgettable adventure.

NOTES:
This challenge is a great way to incorporate many facets of foraging and scouting, not to mention an excellent opportunity to try out some of the other recipes and activities in this book!

Cracking and Shelling Hickory Nuts

Depending on who you ask, there are different ways to go about cracking and shelling hickory nuts. My favorite technique is to combine the two methods below.

THE PROCESS:
Method 1 (courtesy of foraging expert Sam Thayer)

When it comes to hickory nuts, using a nut pick is a waste of time. Instead of freeing large pieces from the shell, the pick tends to pulverize the nutmeat to fine meal. Forager Sam Thayer showed me a better way. The secret lies in cracking the nut correctly in the first place: set the nut on its narrow side and then strike the opposite narrow side (which is facing up) with a hammer.

In order to crack the nut easily, a firm, non-yielding surface beneath it makes a big difference. Sam likes a red oak log; Dave, a friend of mine in Michigan, uses a heavy metal block. A father of one of my former students in Michigan worked in a tool and die shop and gave me a heavy metal block, so that is what I use.

I set the nut on an old washrag or other cloth to keep the nut from sliding on the hard surface when struck with the hammer. I hold the nut between a gloved finger and thumb, being sure to keep my fingers as far down on the nut as possible so I don't bash them with the hammer. The purpose of the glove is less to protect my fingers from being hit by the hammer than it is to reduce "shell shock" as the shell bursts open after being struck. After repeated strikes, these explosions eventually tear up the cloth under the nut. The metal block does a good job of concentrating the impact on the nut.

If the hickory nut has a symmetrical shape, and you strike it just right with a hammer, it should crack into this X-pattern. You can pull off the ends, then the sides, and you can get large pieces of nutmeat – frequently whole halves – this way. With practice, a person can get better and better at it. I've cracked thousands of hickory nuts since Sam showed me his discovery, and I love seeing this perfectly-cracked pattern.

METHOD 2

Ray, a Michigan friend, showed me another clever approach. He uses a vise to crack open the hickory nut. It was definitely slower than Sam's hammer, but less dangerous for a person with less control. Ray modified a 6" pair of diagonal, side-cutting pliers by grinding the head narrower so that it could clip away at the imperfectly cracked shell of hickory nuts. These modified pliers freed larger pieces of nutmeat more rapidly than nut picks. Wanting to have my middle

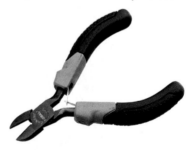

school science classes crack and shell out hickory nuts as an activity, I went shopping for six pairs of diagonal pliers. The 6" diagonal pliers that Ray used were expensive, and I could see that they would require a lot of grinding to make them work. I wasn't looking forward to that. Then I spotted 4-1/2" diagonal pliers with a smaller head that might work without any grinding. They had

Method 2: *After cracking the hickory nut, clip away at the shell to free large pieces of hickory nutmeat.*

cushioned grips, which I judged to be an advantage. The smaller pliers, I reasoned, might work better for the smaller hands of our 7th graders. I bought three different brands so that the students could tell me which they liked best for clipping away the nutshell.

NOTE: Always carefully inspect the hickory nuts you've extracted to make sure they are free of shell shards. One technique to reduce shell shards is to make the shell more flexible before you hit the nut with a hammer. You can do this by soaking a quart of nuts overnight in cold water, or by dropping them into boiling water for two minutes.

Fabulous Fruit Leather
❖ *with Autumn Olives or Chokecherries*

There are three main steps to making any type of fruit leather:

1. Harvest fruit at its prime.

2. Separate pulp and juice from skin, seeds and stems.

3. Halfway through dehydrating the pulp/juice mix, flip over and finish dehydrating.

For this activity, our focus will be on how to make fruit leather out of autumn olives and chokecherries.

RECOGNIZING AUTUMN OLIVES AT THEIR PRIME
Drupes are red and nearly round. They are swollen so much that the dried flower parts on the bottom appear sunken, like a belly button. They taste sour, without a mouth-drying, astringent aftertaste. If the aftertaste is strong, forget that bush and collect from one that tastes better. For more on how to correctly identify ripe autumn olives, see the autumn olive plant profile on page 22.

RECOGNIZING CHOKECHERRIES AT THEIR PRIME
Chokecherries can vary greatly from one shrub to the next in terms of taste. Color may not be helpful, as ripe chokecherries may be red, deep purple or black. A key in determining whether chokecherries are at their prime and ready to harvest is how they separate from the cluster. If they can be easily rolled off between thumb and forefinger, they may have lost most of their astringency and be ready to pick. A taste test will tell you whether to leave them for another week or harvest them now. For more on how to correctly identify ripe chokecherries, see the chokecherries plant profile on page 34.

SOME DEHYDRATING BASICS
The fruit pulp and juice mix (or purée) can be dried to fruit leather in the sun, in an oven, or in a dehydrator. The more surface area you can expose to the heat, the better, so large, shallow trays work best. Some people like to simmer the purée up to an hour

first, to reduce the liquid and cut the drying time in half. I worry about altering the flavor and getting it so dry that it scorches and burns, ruining the time that I've invested. Slower is a safer approach. While cooking helps to get rid of astringency in chokecherries, I prefer the raw, fresh to slightly over-ripe product. Because fruit has sugars that turn to syrup and become very sticky upon evaporation, it's important to loosen and flip the drying fruit leather before it becomes cemented to the tray. Cutting it into sections that can be flipped over with a spatula is helpful.

THE PROCESS:

1. Preheat the oven (or set your dehydrator) to 140° F.

2. Wipe or spray a vegetable oil coating on your baking sheet for the oven or for sun drying outdoors, to lessen sticking. Do the same if you are using the thin, flexible, solid plastic sheets designed for making fruit leather in a dehydrator. As an alternative, lay a sheet of parchment paper over the pan and fold up the edges to contain the fruit purée. If using round plastic dehydrator sheets, set one on top

Processing autumn olives with a food strainer.

of parchment paper as a guide and trim the paper to fit with a pair of scissors.

3. Separate the pulp and juice (see Notes below) OR mix the pulp and juice together to produce a purée. Use a spatula to spread the fruit purée to 1/4" thickness.

4. **a. If you are making fruit leather indoors:** Dehydrate the puree in the oven or dehydrator for 10 hours or until the proper dryness is achieved. Start to check it after 2–3 hours for proper dryness before it can be flipped over. If you gently press down

with a knuckle and mush comes up, more drying is required. When it is done, the fruit leather should look translucent and its surface should feel slightly sticky.

4. **b. If you are making fruit leather outside:** Take a look at the tray after it's been out in the sun for 3-4 hours. If the top feels sticky to the touch, loosen the edges with a spatula, place another baking sheet on top of it and flip the trays. The fruit leather – still somewhat moist on the bottom, but now with the bottom facing up – should drop cleanly onto  the new tray with a little coaxing from a spatula if you are lucky and have timed it just right. You can finish drying it in the sun. If there isn't enough sunlight remaining, bring the tray inside overnight.

5. If you wind up with the fruit leather seemingly glued to your pan or to your dehydrating tray, don't despair. Try this solution: freeze the tray just until the food is frozen, then remove the fruit leather. (Advice from Mary Bell, in *Mary Bell's Complete Dehydrator Cookbook*)

NOTES:

Autumn olive tip: Another way to proceed if you are dealing with autumn olive fruit is to let the reddish-pink pulp and the yellow-tinted juice separate. Pour off the juice, sweeten it to taste, and refrigerate. (It makes a potent, lip-smacking lemonade substitute.) Measure the pulp and mix into it an equal amount of unsweetened applesauce. Dehydrate this into fruit leather. The pectin in the applesauce helps it hold together when removing it from the evaporating tray, and yields a softer, easier to chew fruit leather.

If you plan to go to bed before the dehydration is done, turn off the oven or unplug the dehydrator, or bring the trays indoors overnight. Resume the following day when you can watch it and not let it go too far, which would ruin all your effort.

How to Process Acorns

Conventional wisdom is that acorns from the white oak family (whose leaves have rounded lobes) will have less tannin and taste better than acorns from the red oak family (whose leaves have pointed lobes). That may be true if you are eating them raw, but if you are leaching the acorns, it makes no difference. In fact, I have found that it takes only half as long to leach the bitter-tasting tannins out of fresh red oak acorns than it does out of fresh bur oak acorns. Bur oak is a type of white oak.

GOOD ACORNS, BAD ACORNS

Good acorns to collect have three things in common: they are abundant, large enough to be worth shelling out, and few of them contain grubs of the acorn weevil. Bad acorns are the opposite. If you gather bad acorns, you will have to either toss them or pare away weevil-damaged parts with a knife. From personal experience, I can tell you it quickly becomes frustrating and tedious; however, our aquarium fish loved the weevils!

THE PROCESS:

1. Collect the acorns and avoid weevils

The best way to reduce the number of weevil-damaged acorns you gather is to collect the second or third time the acorns drop from a tree. The second or third drop is discoverable by observation, and even easier to spot if you sweep or rake acorns from the first drop away from the area. Damaged acorns tend to drop first, so any acorns from 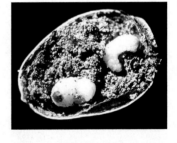 subsequent droppings are usually good. The second or third drop is easy for me to tell as oaks overhang my back porch, parking area, and driveway. A major acorn drop has the same rhythm as popcorn popping. A few fall intermittently, then a wind comes and they sound like a hailstorm in progress.

Another way to avoid weevil-damaged acorns is to be aware of how many damaged acorns you find under particular trees. For example, there's a bur oak in Michigan where practically every acorn has weevils. I avoid it. I discovered a white oak, also in Michigan, that never has weevil-damaged acorns.

The best reference guide to learning to recognize evidence that weevils may be inside an acorn that you pick up is *Nature's Garden: A Guide to Identifying, Harvesting, and Preparing Edible Wild Plants,* by Sam Thayer. It has color photos showing the clues. Take a quick look at acorns before you drop them in your collecting bucket. Reject any that have weevil signs or look blemished.

Another method is to pour your collection into a tub of water and stir. Most of the damaged acorns will float. Skim them off and toss them. Repeat until none float to the top. Spread the good ones out on a tarp to dry in the sun, but watch out for squirrels! They will assume that you are doing this for them.

2. Crack and shell the acorns

Sam Thayer discovered that acorns crack and shell out easier if heated first. To do this, put small batches in a colander and dip them into boiling water for 20 seconds. While the acorns are still warm, crack them gently with a seafood cracker, nutcracker or pliers, and peel off the loose skin.

3. Leach out the tannins (fastest method):
- Put one cup of shelled acorns in a blender. Fill the blender with water, and fasten the top on securely.

- Blend for two minutes.

- Pour contents into a dishtowel-lined colander that has been placed in the sink.

- Run cold water at a rate that won't overflow. Stir the mixture with a wooden spoon for 7 minutes. Turn off the water.

- Let the water drain out of the colander, and then taste a pinch of the acorn meal. If it tastes bitter/acrid, keep running the water and stirring. Check every 2 minutes until the bitterness is gone. I've had fresh red oak acorns that took 7 minutes to get to that stage. Fresh bur oak took 15 minutes, and freshly collected white oak about 12.

One cup of shelled acorn meats yields nearly a cup of acorn meal. See my acorn meal recipe for BABWA Quick Bread on page 130.

STORAGE

As processed above, the acorn meal will resemble damp sand. Gather up the edges of the dishtowel and wring as much water out of the meal as possible. Use it immediately in recipes by adding it to damp ingredients; keep it in your refrigerator for up to a week; or freeze it in flattened heavy-duty freezer bags. If you vacuum seal and freeze the meal, it will keep for up to 4 years. My technique is to pour 2 cups of meal into a quart vacuum seal bag, flatten the bag with my hands, and then vacuum seal the bag. The reason for the 2-cup amount is that none of my recipes require more than 2 cups. Flattening the bag helps the acorns freeze faster, takes up less room in storage and thaws out more quickly when I want to use them.

NOTES:

Acorn meal: dry vs. wet

Acorn nut meal can be dried in the oven or on a sheet in a dehydrator, then ground to finer and finer particle sizes in a blender. After doing that for several years, I decided to experiment. I pitted the damp, sand-particle size acorn meal against the dried, finely ground cornmeal-particle size product in a taste test. The results weren't even close. The wet meal won by a mile. Since then, I don't bother drying and grinding wet acorn meal. I simply package and freeze it. Even if the results had gone the other way, it would be important to package and freeze the dried acorn meal. The reason is that the nut meal is high in fats and oils, and fats and oils can turn rancid at room temperature.

HOW MUCH ACORN MEAL IN A RECIPE?

A few of my foraging friends like to use straight acorn meal, but that makes a dense, heavy product with a taste that I regard as so-so. I prefer one part acorn meal to three or four parts of flour. A small proportion is enough to flavor and darken bread. Since acorns lack gluten, too much interferes with the bread's rising if it's yeast-raised. Yeast-raised acorn products get my vote for superior taste and texture.

How to Process Black Walnuts

Since black walnut trees are so common, I'm often asked how to best go about making good use of them. Many people know that there is a process to collecting and using black walnuts, since you can't eat them right out of the shell, but they're just not sure what the process is.

THE PROCESS:

1. Put on boots and disposable vinyl or latex gloves.

2. To husk black walnuts, step on them where they have fallen on the ground, twisting your foot to pop the husk off. Toss them in a 5-gallon bucket with your gloved hands.

3. Pour a gallon or so of the husked nuts into a wire fish basket.

4. Tie or clip the basket to something, then stand back and use the power washer to clean the walnuts off.

5. Dry your clean walnuts outdoors on a tarp, but remember to pull them inside a garage or shed when you plan to be away from home, so that you don't share the cleaned walnuts with squirrels. I spread the tarp out in my garage and set a fan up to blow over them for a couple of days until they are good and dry.

6. Store them in a 6-to-10 gallon galvanized trashcan with a bail that locks the lid – it keeps any mice from rolling the nuts around your house! Wait a couple of weeks for them to cure before cracking and using them.

7. To crack the walnuts, use a shop vise or even a hammer. Find more tips on page 105, Cracking Hickory Nuts. Diagonal (side-cutting) pliers help snip away some of the partitions to make it simpler to get large pieces free with a nut pick. Once the nutmeats are extracted, they keep best in the freezer as they are quite oily and the oils can become rancid at room temperature.

See page 137 for my Cinnamon Black Walnut Ice Cream recipe. It's a favorite!

NOTES:

If your back starts hurting from all the bending and picking up, or you have more than two trees' worth of walnuts to gather (or you just want to speed the collection process), I highly recommend purchasing a large Nut Wizard®. See photo right for what the Nut Wizard looks like.

As Josh Price rolls this long-handled Nut Wizard over the walnuts, the spring wires are forced apart, and then snap shut as he goes past the walnuts.

Note to leaders: If your youth group is looking for a way to raise money, buying a few Nut Wizards could prove to be a good investment. Property owners might be willing to pay to have their walnuts picked up every fall. It wouldn't take long to recoup your investment. There are cheaper imitations on the market that don't work as well nor last as long. Nut Wizard is the original and the best. I recommend watching the YouTube videos at NutWizard.com. Seeds and Such, Inc., is the distributor.

   If you are looking for hulling stations, Hammon's is the world's largest processor of black walnuts, shelling about 25 million pounds a year. Hammon's sends trucks all over the Midwest and East Central U.S. to pick up black walnuts from their black walnut hulling stations. Simply go to their website, black-walnuts.com, and enter a zip code to find the address of the nearest hulling station. There's also a state-by-state listing where you can find the names of the stores that sell Hammon's shelled black walnuts. You can order them online, too, but they cost more as you have to pay for shipping. Their Facebook page, HammonsBlackWalnuts, is a good place to find mouth-watering, seasonally appropriate recipes.

Mushroom Foray and Tasting

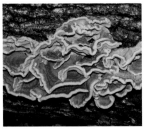
You've just read the top half of a sign-up sheet for a workshop that I conducted during the Midwest Wild Harvest Festival. This popular wild food gathering takes place the second weekend of September at the Wisconsin Badger Camp, about 10 miles south of Prairie du Chien in southwestern Wisconsin. 145 participants are considered the carrying capacity of the MWHF, and 145 people signed up before the middle of August. Twenty-five were allowed into the mushrooming workshop, and I was fortunate to have Damian Pieper's assistance. Damian, once president of Iowa's Prairie States Mushroom Club, can recognize many of the commonly found mushrooms. Rachel Mifsud, a biology lecturer for the University of Michigan, Dearborn, helped out on the foray.

I will describe our foray and workshop, thinking that it could serve as a template for successful group forays you may want to organize, large or small.

THE PROCESS:
The Foray

A foray is a mushroom hunt that includes at least a few knowledgeable people. It typically lasts a couple of hours. You might set your starting time at 10:00 on a Saturday morning to allow people who work during the week, and who may have to drive a ways, to join you. The site could be a picnicking area in a park, recreation area, or on private land, where collecting mushrooms is permitted. The idea would be to wander off in small groups, adding mushrooms to your baskets, and then return to the starting point at noon. You could spread your find out on dedicated picnic tables, leaving room on other tables for a sack lunch. After washing your hands, you'd get your sack lunch and beverage out of the car, along with mushroom identification books if you have them, and find a spot to sit and socialize with others as you enjoy lunch. After lunch, those who know about the mushrooms could share their knowledge of the find. Photographs could be taken. A list of species is often compiled, and later shared on a website. By typing the mushroom's scientific name into a Google Images search, you can be reminded of what the mushroom looks like. Positively identified edible mushrooms could be taken home by those who wish to cook them up. The rest of the mushrooms should be cleaned off the picnic table and scattered back in the woods.

Our foray was similar to this in many respects, but it had differences. It was part of a 4-hour afternoon workshop. We had already eaten lunch. We didn't develop a list of species. We focused on two things: how to identify a mushroom with a field guide, and the unadulterated taste of some of fall's finest edible mushrooms.

AFTER THE FORAY:
Identifying, Cooking and Tasting

Returning from the foray, we spread our find out on picnic tables. I provided multiple copies of Kuo and Methven's *Mushrooms of the Midwest* and spoke briefly about the process of identifying an unknown with the help of a good reference book. I split the group up, taking some to start cooking mushrooms for everyone to taste, while Damian worked with the rest on using the reference to identify mushrooms.

Maggie Kwong Taylor, right foreground, from the Dragon House Restaurant in Columbia Heights, MN, cooked mushrooms with butter and oyster sauce.

A mushroom bounty. Prior to the MWHF, I placed posts on Facebook, asking those planning to attend to kindly bring edible mushrooms for us to cook and taste in my workshop, and got a great response. We were able to refrigerate and retrieve an adequate supply of ten species: sulfur shelf, oyster, elm oyster, yellow oyster, hen of the woods, lion's mane, common chanterelle, slippery jack, pear-shaped puffball, and giant puffball. No Scotch bonnets; last year there were thousands of them in the tenting site. (One woman, unknowingly, even pitched her tent inside a fairy ring of them!) And we had no shaggymane, inky caps, honey mushrooms, aborted entolomas or wood ears, other edibles that make fall a fabulous time for hunting mushrooms.

We fried up individual trays of different species, and then invited Damian's group to join our taste-testing party. Each mushroom was fried in grapeseed oil and drained on paper toweling.

NOTES:

Find out if there are any programs like the one described above going on near you. Joining a mushroom club and going on forays with the members is a great way to increase your confidence. The North American Mycological Association has contact information for affiliated clubs by state, by region, and by Canadian province. Check this link: http://www.namyco.org/clubs.php.

Persimmon Taste Test

Just the thought of a persimmon taste test makes me smile. Unripe persimmons are astringent. They dry your mouth so fast that the experience is unforgettable. You pucker up immediately! Every person should encounter an unripe persimmon at least once in a lifetime. If you decide to try this on a relative or friend, warn them ahead of time so they won't seek revenge. (They will probably want to taste it anyway, like our Scout troop did.)

THE PROCESS:

1. Grab two containers.

2. Go out and find a persimmon tree (bring your containers!)

3. Once you've found a persimmon tree, start collecting persimmons. In one container, put only persimmons that are orange, nice-looking and smooth-skinned; these will be picked off the tree. In the other container, put only orange persimmons that are wrinkled and have fallen on the ground.

4. Present your two containers to your victims. Have them guess which container holds the ripe persimmons. Then, encourage them to try persimmons from each container. The nice-looking, smooth ones from the tree are still unripe and strongly astringent; the wrinkled ones from the ground are ripe and delicious.

5. Try not to smile as you wait to see their reactions.

NOTES:

I learned to judge ripeness the hard way, by taste-testing. Here's what I discovered:

- The persimmon must be on the ground, or easily shaken from the tree.
- The persimmon must not be attached to a twig that has fallen.
- The persimmon must feel soft and look wrinkled.
- The stiff, dark brown calyx, if still attached, will twist off with hardly any resistance.

If tasted, the persimmon will taste sweet, with no bitter or puckery aftertaste.

Ripe persimmons are a wonderful snack food on a hike.

These 5 persimmons, found on the ground, were still attached to twigs. Although the one in the lower left corner feels soft and is starting to get wrinkled, because it is still attached to the twig, consider it unripe and look for others. If you doubt this statement, a taste test will convince you. Remember: fully ripe persimmons do not cling to the twig!

Preparing Dandelions for Cooking and Baking

Dandelions are notorious for their bitter taste. It comes from a group of chemicals called sesquiterpenes that are found in the milky juice of the plant. There are four things we can do about that and still benefit from the amazing nutrition dandelions offer: we can reduce the bitterness, dilute it, mask it, or overpower it.

In the case of dandelion flowers – the star ingredient in the recipes for Dandelion Donuts and Dandy Burgers – reducing the bitterness is the way to go. Thanks to insight from Dr. Peter Gail, who may know more about dandelions than anyone else in the world, we can actually remove the bitterness from the flowers. Our concept of a flower includes not only the actual flower or flower head but also its base and the stem. Now here's the secret: the bitterness isn't found in the yellow flower head of a dandelion flower; it is found in the green base right under the yellow ray flowers and also in the hollow stem. That means to get rid of the bitterness we only need to separate the yellow flower part from the green base and stem. We keep the yellow and compost the rest.

This can be accomplished with a snip from a pair of sharp scissors or a slice from a paring knife. But wait! There is a safer, more effective way to separate yellow from green, and with practice it becomes more accurate and almost as fast as scissors or a paring knife. Dr. Gail developed, practiced and refined this technique and taught it to me.

THE PROCESS:
1. Start by picking yourself a small practice bowl of dandelion flowers with about an inch of stem left on each one. The inch of stem makes it easier to remove the yellow part, so while it is simpler to pluck the dandelion from the lawn by pulling up on the flower, doing so breaks off the stem right under the green base. Consequently, it won't work as well.

2. Pinch the dandelion's green base between your thumb and forefinger.

Dandelion Squeezing Team *With a little practice, Keokuk Middle School students Kurstin Brown, Steven Masterson and Michael Brennan became proficient in separating the non-bitter yellow flowers from the bitter green parts below the flowers.*

3. Gradually increase the pressure between your forefinger and your thumb as you squeeze down on the green flower base.

4. When it feels like the flowers in the flower head have come loose, you should be able to easily pull them free with the fingers of your other hand and drop them into an empty bowl.

Now you're ready to make Dandelion Donuts (page 138) and Dandy Burgers (page 141)!

The Sumac Lemonade Challenge

For 20 years, my 7th grade science students learned experimenting skills by trying to solve this problem: how can we make consistently good-looking and good-tasting sumac lemonade?

When we first started, it wasn't unusual for me to get an alarmed call from a parent. At the supper table, the question had been asked of their son or daughter "What did you do in science today?" Parents had heard of poison sumac and wanted to be reassured that I wasn't going to endanger their son or daughter. I carefully explained that we were using only the red-berried sumacs; poison sumac had white berries. I further assured them that every edible wild plant book I owned said that red-berried sumacs were safe; some even suggested how to make sumac lemonade – though none of them made consistently good-looking and good-tasting sumac lemonade.

And so our research began. We formed and tested hypotheses. We controlled and manipulated variables. Tasting samples helped us know whether we were on the right track. Some of the looks on students' faces when they sipped the latest experiment were priceless! We made progress every year, with the sumac lemonade looking better and tasting better.

Finally, after 20 years of research conducted by many classes, we arrived at two ways that were voted equal in appearance and taste. Drum roll, please! You'll find the winning recipes on pages 160 and 161.

HERE IS WHAT WE LEARNED FROM SUMAC LEMONADE RESEARCH

Problem statement: Discover how to make consistently good looking and good tasting sumac lemonade.

Research Findings

1. The best looking and best tasting sumac lemonade is made from sumac fruit heads that:

   a. are uniformly dark red to bright red in color.

   b. have drupes whose coating tastes super-sour. (To tell, rub a few drupes between thumb and forefinger and lick the residue left on your fingers. We defined "super-sour" as "sour enough to cause you to make a face, but then relax into a smile as the sourness seems pleasant, and not harsh.")

      1) As the fruit heads ripen over the season, rains will wash away the acids responsible for the sour taste. The taste will progress through four stages: unpleasantly sour, super-sour, sour, and barely sour. A key finding of our research is that the only stage that produces consistently good looking and good tasting sumac lemonade is the super-sour stage.

   c. is made from de-stemmed, then shaken, drupes. The fastest way to remove the drupes from their attachment to the tiny stems in the fruit cluster is to make the stemlets brittle by drying them first. Let them air dry for several days or load a baking pan up with sumac fruit heads and bake it for 20 minutes at 300° F. Take a fruit head in one hand with the top facing away from you, and a fruit head in the other hand with the top facing toward you. Rub them against each other over a bowl to catch the falling drupes. Put the de-stemmed drupes in a kitchen strainer. Shake the strainer from side to side over a wastebasket to clean them without using water. This allows the dried flower petals (which have turned brown), broken pieces of stems, and any insect poop to fall through the mesh of the strainer. All of these would have given the lemonade a brownish color. Pick out any small clusters of broken stemlets for the same reason.

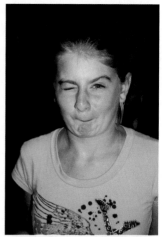

2. Sumac fruit clusters ripen between mid-July and early October. Those in the same group of shrubs will ripen at the same time, as sumac grows in clonal patches. Other patches may have a different ripening time. The only way to tell is with a taste test. When a sumac fruit head begins to ripen, it will be a mix of red and green drupes, and the stemlets will be green. Eventually, the whole head will become dark, wet and intensely sour. For a week or two, the heads are often partially coated with a white, sour to sweet, waxy glaze reminiscent of the glaze on glazed donuts. At this stage, they can be acid enough to burn the lips of sensitive people. Another concern is that the stems are too flexible, making it harder to remove the drupes. Our hands get covered with a reddish, incredibly sour-tasting residue that is hairy in the case of staghorn sumac. It washes off easily. While fruit heads at this stage can be used, it

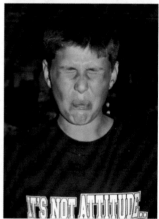

Top: a "super-sour" reaction; Bottom: an "unpleasantly-sour" reaction to sumac drupes

is easier to wait a month and work with clusters that are drier. The drupes roll off the tiny stems of the cluster with ease, and the super-sour taste produces a more agreeable drink than the incredibly sour, just-ripened drupes.

3. Since the super-sour content of the drupes is water soluble, rain can leach the sourness out of the fruit clusters. In keeping track of two sumac stands whose fruit ripened in early September, I found that short rains, even if heavy, had little effect. All day rains, however, leached the sourness right out of the heads.

4. Critters such as jumping spiders, stink bugs, caterpillars, and plant bugs are more likely to be found inside older fruit clusters. As their frass (poop) also is more likely in older fruit clusters, particularly those of the fuzzy staghorn sumac, it's worthwhile to keep an eye on when specific clusters begin to ripen, and time your harvest before the bugs invade.

5. It is not necessary to mash or crush the clusters of sumac, nor soak them for long periods of time in order to extract the flavor. In fact, the stems, stemlets and seeds contain tannins that can impart bitterness to the sumac lemonade and give it a brownish tint. The desirable red color and flavor come from the coating of each drupe. This includes the skin and the hairs. The hairs on staghorn sumac are large and transparent. With a binocular/dissecting microscope, one can see the red pigment and acid inside the hollow hairs.

Staghorn sumac – note the large hairs covering the drupes

Toasted Silver Maple Keys

Widely planted because they are rapidly growing shade trees, silver maples have one drawback: they produce thousands of seeds (inside their keys) that spin down like helicopters to start a forest in your lawn. Until I traveled to a weekend gathering of foragers, I had found no good way to make use of silver maple seeds. Green, shelled out of their keys and cooked, they still seemed bitter to my taste, possibly due to the tannins they contain. I tried leaching the tannins out as one might do for acorns, with multiple changes of water, but found no improvement. Finally, serendipity! At that foragers weekend, Diane Schrum, a Facebook friend, shared toasted silver maple keys. Find her process on the following page.

Diane Schrum with toasted silver maple keys

DIANE'S PROCESS:

1. In mid-spring before the squirrels do their civic duty, grab a small container and go find the closest silver maple tree. Collect the fresh fallen keys or grab some from easy-to-reach branches with hundreds of green seed clusters. Don't take squishy ones or those with black dots or a grayish hue!

2. Take the keys home and remove the stems from the clusters.

3. Toss the keys with your favorite oil (I used 1/2 cup of peanut oil).

4. Spread the keys out on a tray and bake them at 375° F for about 20–40 minutes until they start popping and are golden brown. A convection oven works best for this. Halfway through, turn and stir the seeds and give them a brief sprinkle of sea salt (or sugar!)

5. After the keys are toasted, remove them from the baking sheet and allow them to cool on a tray covered with paper towels. Use another paper towel to gently blot up excess oil.

NOTES:

If you're looking for something a little sweeter, toss the keys with a sprinkling of sugar instead of sea salt at the halfway point. You can store the keys by pouring them into a container and keeping them refrigerated. Warm the keys up in a frying pan after refrigeration and serve!

Recipes

Several of the recipes here have won national acclaim; all have been requested multiple times by those who have tasted them. If you are a beginner when it comes to cooking wild edibles, may these serve as a confidence-building springboard to further culinary adventures. If you are a skilled cook, may you find suggestions that will get your creative juices flowing and delight your family and friends.

BABWA Quick Bread
❖ *(Banana-Acorn-Black Walnut-Apple)*
Yield: one 9" loaf

Accompanied with spreadables like honey butter, mayapple marmalade and wild grape jelly, this bread took first place at the annual meeting of the National Wild Foods Association.

THE RECIPE:
1 package Pillsbury® Banana Quick Bread Mix*
1/2 cup processed acorn meal
1/2 cup black walnuts (one 2-oz. pkg. at store)
1/2 cup grated apple (1 medium-large or 2 small apples)
1 cup water
1/4 cup oil
3 eggs (Vegan substitute: 3 tablespoons milled flax seed
plus 9 tablespoons water)

1. Preheat oven to 375° F and grease and flour the bottom (only) of a 9" non-stick loaf pan.

2. Add ingredients to a large mixing bowl, then beat 60–75 strokes by hand.

3. Pour into a prepared loaf pan. Cover with an aluminum foil tent to prevent a split top.

4. Bake 50–60 minutes, until a toothpick inserted in the center comes out clean. Let cool 15 minutes in pan, then loosen edges and tilt out onto a cooling rack. The bread crumbles easily, so handle it gently.

Can be refrigerated up to one week or wrapped in freezer paper** and frozen up to three months.

NOTES:
Wild apples were used in making the winning entry, as one of the criteria for judging was wild food content. However, the apples don't need to be wild.

By substituting Pillsbury Pumpkin Quick Bread Mix, you can create PABWA Quick Bread, also quite tasty.

**Residual tannin/tannic acid in the bread will react with the aluminum in the foil. Some aluminum may be dissolved and might give a sensitive person a headache. Better to avoid any problems by using freezer paper, or plastic wrap before aluminum foil.*

Burdock Kinpira
Yield: 3 cups

I first sampled this delightful Japanese side dish at the Whole Foods Deli in Ann Arbor, Michigan, decades ago. Found it so good that I frequently checked back to learn when I might purchase more. The chef was reluctant to divulge the recipe until I explained that it was to be applied to my edible wild plant hobby, where I sought great recipes to use with edible wild plants such as the invasive and despised burdock. He didn't want me competing with the Deli, and I promised him that I would not. After making several batches from wild burdock, here is my slight alteration of the procedure, which has stood the test of time and received favorable reviews from all who have tasted it.

THE RECIPE:
2 cups matchstick-sized pieces of first-year burdock taproots
   (First-year plants have no flowering stalk. You will likely need two or three roots, depending on their size. Dig with care, as the very long taproots are easily broken. Compost piles or sandy soils offer the easiest digging.)
1 cup matchstick-sized pieces of carrots
1 tablespoon toasted sesame oil
1 cup water
1 tablespoon sesame seeds
2 tablespoons tamari soy sauce
1 tablespoon honey

As this is a stir-fry recipe, you'll want a wok. Mine didn't come with a lid, so I use a large frying pan lid when simmering and steaming in step 3. Whether I'm using a carbon steel wok, a non-stick wok, or an electric wok, I prefer a large wooden spoon for stirring.

1. Scrub and peel burdock roots. Split burdock roots in half lengthwise. Strip out and discard any woody cores. Cut burdock and carrots into matchstick-sized pieces.

2. In the wok, stir-fry burdock, carrot and sesame seed in sesame oil for 3-4 minutes

3. Add the water. Bring to a boil, then cover and turn heat down, simmering and steaming for 15 minutes.

4. Remove lid. Mix soy sauce and honey together and pour over the burdock and carrots in the wok.

5. Turn the heat up. Stir until all the liquid is absorbed for best flavor.

Cattail Vegetarian Pulled-Pork Barbecue

Yield: 3-4 cups

I love going to wild food weekends. Each offers an opportunity to gather and taste new wild foods while in different parts of the country and to learn from foragers who enjoy experimenting with processing techniques and recipes.

One of the food items that surprised me at a Nature Wonder Wild Foods Weekend in West Virginia was a mock pulled-pork barbecue made from the brown seed heads of cattail. The cattail heads were collected in mid-September. The texture and taste were astonishingly realistic and so tasty that I requested the recipe. The original recipe is by Erin Froehlich (see Notes). I've done a little rewording on the procedure and have doubled the amount of onion, based on our experience in following it, but the ingredients she chose and the technique she developed is a discovery worth sharing. Thanks, Erin!

THE RECIPE:

2 cups brown cattail fluff

3 eggs

1/2 cup melted butter (Erin used vegan butter; real butter works fine.)

1/8 cup milk (Erin used almond milk; any milk should work just as well.)

2 tablespoons real maple syrup

1 teaspoon nutmeg

1 teaspoon black pepper

1 medium red onion

Hickory barbecue sauce (or your choice)

1. Preheat oven to 275° F.

2. Loosen cattail fluff from the stem core: place 2 dark brown cattail heads in a plastic shopping bag. Tie the handles of the bag together as you squeeze out the air. Wrap your hands around one of the cattails from outside the bag, and twist your hands in opposite directions to separate the seeds and fluff from the knitting-needle-like core of the cattail head. Repeat. (Try to keep the fluff contained, or you'll have seeds drifting all over the place!) Carefully transfer two moderately-packed cups of seed fluff into a medium sized-mixing bowl.

3. Stir in the eggs, melted butter, maple syrup, nutmeg and black pepper with the cattail fluff. Once thoroughly combined, transfer mixture to a food processor.

4. Blend well in food processor, adding the milk to help smooth it out. Pour into a greased 8 x 8" baking dish and spread evenly.

5. Bake in a 275° F oven for about 20 minutes or until rising bubbles occur and the mixture starts to puff up. Remove from oven. Let cool for a while, then cut into thirds one way and fourths the other way.

6. As you remove each rectangle, tear it into pieces roughly one inch in size and place them into a small bowl. Set aside.

7. Dice a medium sized onion and toss in a skillet over medium high heat. Sprinkle generously with black pepper and cook until onion pieces have caramelized but are still moist.

8. Dump the "pulled pork" pieces in with the onions and cook until mixture is hot.

9. Stir in your favorite BBQ sauce. Enjoy!

NOTES:

If you go to www.smartliving network.com/food/b/gastronomics-foraged-cattail-vegetarian-pulled-pork-barbeque-recipe/, you will find an illustrated and intriguing account of how Erin created her recipe.)

On the web page where Erin posted her recipe, someone asked the question, "...how late in the season can you actually use the fluff? Does it get too fibrous as it gets closer to bursting open? Or can you use the brown 'heads' at any stage?"

My reply: "In February, from a marsh where some of the narrow-leaved cattail *(Typha angustifolia)* heads were still brown and compact, but more had already exploded into a fluffy white and brown seed head, I collected the compact brown heads only. Using your recipe, they worked fine. I tried the fluffy white and brown seed heads this week (1st wk. of March.) The flavor was excellent, but I had to spit out wads of fibers with every bite."

FURTHER TESTING:

Narrow-leaved cattail seedheads that were more greenish than brown in August were collected and tried, using Erin's recipe. The heads were so tightly packed and tightly attached that it was very difficult to remove the developing seeds and fluff from the knitting-needle-like core. No seeds became airborne on fluff, as happens later in the year. The barbecue taste was there, but it was hard to chew, and definitely too fibrous.

Collected from the same location the second week of September. The heads were definitely browner, but still somewhat greenish. Easier to remove seeds and the pre-fluff, but alas, it is still tough and fibrous to eat. Found another location where the seedheads were all brown, and they produced a less fibrous result. Had several tiny seeds drifting around the room on their fluff. They came off the core very easily, so we resorted to putting the heads in a plastic shopping bag to contain them, as we twisted the seeds and fluff loose.

From my testing, I would conclude that the prime time to collect cattail heads is when they are a dark chocolate brown, and before the heads begin to break apart.

Cinnamon Black Walnut Ice Cream

Yield: one gallon

This recipe, adapted from the Rival® Electric Ice Cream Maker Owner's Guide, is a delicious showcase for those black walnuts you have collected.

THE RECIPE:
1 quart whipping cream
1 quart half and half
2 cups sugar
1 tablespoon vanilla extract
1 teaspoon cinnamon
1/2 teaspoon salt
2-1/2 cups chopped black walnuts

1. Combine all ingredients except black walnuts. Cover and refrigerate for 30 minutes.

2. Place the black walnuts in a separate container and refrigerate.

3. After the mix has been chilled, pour it into the cylinder of an ice cream maker. Make the ice cream and transfer it to a storage container.

4. Using a wooden spoon, fold in the walnuts while the ice cream is still soft.

NOTES:
The flavor improves after several days of storage in a freezer, if you can wait that long!

Dandelion Donuts

Yield: approximately 40 donuts

Perhaps the most-remembered wild food activity in our Scout troop and in 7th grade science is when we collected, prepared and ate dandelion donuts. For the benefit of Scouts and my former students, here's my famous but simple recipe. Thought you might want to share it with your children and grandchildren. I've included a few things we learned along the way.

If you have any flowers left over, head to page 141 for something a little more savory: Dandy Burgers!

BEFORE YOU START:

Separate the yellow dandelion flowers from their bitter-tasting green base and stem until you have 1 cup of yellow flowers. For detailed instructions on how to do this, see page 121, Preparing Dandelions for Cooking and Baking. Remember to compost the base and stem.

As you are preparing the dandelions, begin heating the cooking oil to 375° F in an electric frying pan. Whether it was in my classroom or in our Scout meeting room, while one group was squeezing freshly picked dandelion flowers, another group would begin heating up the cooking oil. We used about 2 quarts of oil in a 12"-square electric pan.

THE RECIPE:

2 cups Bisquick® Baking Mix
2 eggs
1 cup milk
1 cup yellow dandelion flowers
Cooking oil
Cinnamon, sugar or powdered sugar

1. In a stainless steel, glass or ceramic bowl (not plastic), mix together the Bisquick mix, eggs and milk. Stir in the flowers.

In their 7th grade science classroom at Keokuk Middle School, Rachel Carman, Allison Leach and Zach Benedict demonstrate the setup we use when making dandelion donuts.

2. Gently drop teaspoon-sized balls of dough into the hot cooking oil. The oil is hot enough when a teaspoon of batter sinks, bubbles along the edges and immediately bobs back up to the surface. Do only 6 at a time so that the cooking oil doesn't cool off and start soaking into the donut. Turn the donuts when light golden brown on the underside.

3. Drain on paper towels. Roll in sugar, cinnamon and sugar, or powdered sugar.

TIPS:

We used a stainless steel bowl for batter (a lesson learned after melting a plastic one against the hot electric frying pan); two long-handled teaspoons to scrape and ease a teaspoonful of batter into the hot oil; a chef's long-handled slotted nylon spoon to gently roll the donuts over and to remove them to a paper towel lined baking sheet when they were done; three loaf pans, one with a cup of plain sugar, one with a cup of powdered sugar, and the last with a cup of a mix of cinnamon and sugar. When the freshly fried donuts were cool enough to handle, a third cook would shake them in a loaf pan to sugar them. Finally, the sugared donuts were placed on top of a baking sheet lined with a clean paper towel. That baking sheet was carried around the room to serve the donuts when we finished cooking.

WAIT, THESE DON'T LOOK LIKE DONUTS!

That's true; they don't! They look more like doughnut holes. So why don't I call them dandelion donut holes? A donut hole is made from the leftover dough cut out of the middle of a donut. That hasn't happened here. It is not how they are constructed, nor are the ingredients the same. Some doughnuts are yeast raised. Mine are not.

I've heard them called dandelion fritters. Fritters, however, are constructed by dipping a flower in batter, then deep-frying it. Some foragers (including me once upon a time) have picked a dandelion flower head, dipped it in batter, and then deep fried it and called it a donut. It is a fritter and not a donut. I stopped making them that way years ago when I had several sensitive people get sick from eating the bitter green receptacle under the yellow flower head.

Some people might suggest that they are French or New Orleans-style beignets. Not true. Beignets are made from different ingredients and are often constructed to have a square shape.

They resemble Portuguese masalas, but masalas use evaporated milk. Mine use fresh milk. Masalas contain no dandelion flowers; mine do.

One friend even took to calling them dandelion hushpuppies. Hushpuppies typically contain cornmeal and chopped onion. My recipe doesn't include either cornmeal or chopped onion.

"Puffs" might be a more accurate, if somewhat nebulous name. Unfortunately, the term makes me think of a brand of facial tissue – so that's out.

Let's just agree to call them donuts. After all, the name "dandelion donuts" has a nice ring to it.

Dandy Burgers

◈ *Tweaking a Prize-Winning Vegetarian Recipe*
Yield: Four 2½"-diameter patties

Dandelion season is the perfect time of the year to try this recipe. Layton Hawkins, one of my former 7th grade science students at Keokuk Middle School, first brought it to my attention. He found it online at backpacker.com and asked if he might fix it in class and get credit on our Dandelions & Lawns Unit. "Absolutely!" I said. I have eaten other dandelion burgers, but this one blows the competition away; I can understand why Dandy Burgers took top prize in a backcountry cooking event.

Before I share the recipe, credit is due to Frank Cetera of Slippery Rock, Pennsylvania, and whoever created the original recipe that Frank found in a newsletter. Frank modified the recipe for backpackers, and entered it in the cooking event sponsored by the Pennsylvania chapter of the North Country Trail Association. The recipe still might not have made it in Backpacker magazine for August, 2000, if it hadn't been for author Susan Newquist and the editors who selected it and have kept its post on backpacker.com all these years. Thank you!

If you want to have burgers that are a little more filling and meaty, my northern Illinois Facebook friend Diane Schrum recommends adding ground-up nuts of your choice to the mix. I decided to experiment with different types of nut meal: acorn, black walnut, hazelnut, hickory nut, and pecan. The acorns were first processed to remove their bitterness. All of the nut meal burgers were good, but I was particularly fond of two of them: the one with hickory nuts and the other with pecans. Mary Frakes, my housekeeper, who enjoys experimenting and cooking, judged the pecan burger the best.

My changes are shown in red italics. To see the original recipe, head to backpacker.com and search "Dandy Burgers."

THE RECIPE:

1/2 teaspoon salt

1/3 cup wheat flour

1/8 teaspoon pepper

1/2 teaspoon garlic powder

1/4 teaspoon dried basil

1/2 teaspoon dried oregano

1/4 cup wheat germ

2 tablespoons ground pecans (or nut meal of your choosing)

1/4 cup powdered milk

1-1/2 tablespoons powdered egg or 1 fresh egg

1 cup fresh-picked dandelion blossoms
    (yellow part only; see page 121)

1/4 cup chopped fresh onion

1/4 cup chopped fresh green onion

1. At home, combine dry ingredients in a zipper lock bag and bring it with you to camp.

2. In camp, where you will prepare the burgers, add the onions, dandelion blossoms and egg (if using fresh) to the zipper lock bag containing the dry ingredients.

3. Knead well into a stiff batter. Using clean hands, shape into patties.

4. Heat the frying pan and fry burgers a few minutes on each side until golden brown but not dried out.

NOTES:

Finding a prize-winning recipe, tasting it, and then experimenting with it can be a lot of fun. As a former teacher, I believe this would be a great homework assignment that kids would enjoy doing. Experimenting with recipes is a useful application of science.

I could also see challenging members of youth groups to create or tweak a recipe that they could fix at their next meeting or on their next camping or canoe trip. It would make an intriguing project or activity. Two ideas: create a meal that can be cooked on a stick; create an original foil dinner.

Double-Good Blueberry Pie
Yield: one 9" pie

Double-Good Blueberry Pie is one of many fond memories I have from 30 years spent living in Michigan. The state is blessed with an abundance of low-bush and high-bush blueberries. Scouts and I eagerly snacked on them for a mouthful of juicy energy while hiking or canoeing. The much larger commercially grown blueberries were like a magnet for me when in season. While getting my pails weighed at a blueberry farm near Howell, I picked up this recipe to try. Quick, easy and bursting with flavor, it immediately became my favorite blueberry pie recipe. I have fixed it on a campout, as the only thing that needs to be baked is the pie shell. The mix of raw blueberries in a cooked blueberry matrix is sensational. That is where it got its double-good name. Try it – you'll like it!

THE RECIPE:
Baked 9" pie shell
3/4 cup sugar
3 tablespoons cornstarch
1/4 teaspoon salt
1/4cup water
4 cups blueberries
1 tablespoon butter
1 tablespoon lemon juice
Whipped cream (optional)

1. Combine sugar, cornstarch and salt in saucepan. Add water and two cups of the blueberries.

2. Cook blueberry mixture over medium heat, stirring constantly, until it comes to a boil and has thickened. It should be a translucent purple and thick.

3. Remove from heat and stir in butter and lemon juice. Cool.

4. Place remaining 2 cups raw blueberries in pie shell. Top with cooked blueberry mixture.

5. Chill. Serve, garnished with whipped cream.

NOTES:

If you go to the effort of gathering wild blueberries, you'll appreciate a recipe that maximizes their flavor, a recipe that will be an instant family favorite, a recipe that company will request again and again. This incredible Great Lakes® blueberry pie recipe is courtesy of and copyrighted by the Michigan Blueberry Growers Association, Grand Junction, MI 49056. Used by permission.

GAZP –
A Garden Weed Quiche!
Yield: one 9-10" quiche (8 servings)

"GAZP" stands for "Goosefoot And Zucchini Pie." It's a simple, crustless quiche I modified from a zucchini pie recipe given me by Sue Schongalla in the late 1970s. Goosefoot or lambsquarters *(Chenopodium album)* is a common garden weed that works particularly well in this easily made pie. Other garden weeds like purslane, chickweed, amaranth and yellow wood sorrel or sheep sorrel may be incorporated. Purslane adds a nice textural note, and the sorrels provide a refreshing sourness.

THE RECIPE:
3 cups grated zucchini
1 cup young, tender goosefoot (lambsquarters) leaf cluster tips
1/2 cup other weeds may be added (purslane, chickweed, amaranth, sheep sorrel, yellow wood sorrel)
1 small onion, chopped
1 cup Bisquick or Jiffy Mix
4 eggs
1/2 cup vegetable oil
1/2 cup shredded Swiss cheese
1/2 cup shredded Colby and Monterey Jack cheeses
Heavy sprinkling of grated Parmesan cheese
1/2 teaspoon dried parsley or several sprigs of fresh parsley with long stems removed
1/2 teaspoon marjoram
1/2 teaspoon salt
1/2 teaspoon pepper
Paprika to sprinkle or sift over the pie before baking
Optional: 1 cup pitted, sliced black olives. (Use 1/2 cup in step 2; 1/2 cup in step 4)

1. Preheat oven to 350° F.
2. Place all ingredients in bowl except zucchini. Mix well. Fold in zucchini.
3. Pour batter into a buttered or oiled 9–10" pie pan. Sprinkle with paprika and extra parsley. Optional: top with sliced black olives.
4. Bake 30–40 minutes. Test with a toothpick; if the toothpick comes out doughy, bake longer, until the toothpick comes out clean.

NOTES:
A delightful lunch, whether served hot or cold.

Microwave Bread & Butter Purslane Pickles

Yield: 1-1/2 cups (12 servings)

While searching for a pickle recipe to use with purslane, I found a simple recipe for microwave bread and butter pickles, by "Linda," on allrecipes.com, 2005. Twenty-seven out of 31 reviewers felt it outstanding, and gave it 5 stars (the highest rating), while a few felt it would be improved with less sugar. In this modification of Linda's well-liked recipe, I cut back on the sugar and onion and substituted purslane stems for the cucumber. I've also tweaked the format, amounts and microwave time, and substituted apple cider vinegar for distilled white vinegar.

I found Linda's recipe delightful on three counts: it makes a small amount, it is incredibly simple to make, and it is delicious. In fact, you may want to try the original, at allrecipes.com.

THE RECIPE:

3 cups purslane stem pieces (they can be up to the thickness of a pencil, but should not feel woody or fibrous when you bend, cut or bite into them. Strip them of their leaves. Cut into 2–3" pieces.)

1 teaspoon salt

1/2 Vidalia onion, thinly sliced

1/2 teaspoon mustard seeds

1/2 cup white sugar

1/2 cup apple cider vinegar

1/4 teaspoon celery seed

1/4 teaspoon ground turmeric

1. Mix everything together and place it in a quart-sized, glass microwavable bowl. Cover with a microwavable lid.

2. Microwave on high for 6–7 minutes, stirring twice at intervals, until purslane is tender and the sliced onion is translucent.

3. Transfer to sterile containers, label and date, and store in the refrigerator for up to three months until ready to eat. (See page 175 for how to sterilize containers.)

Mike's Mayapple Marmalade, v. 4.1

❖ *(with a tip of the hat to Euell Gibbons)*
Yield: six 8-ounce or twelve 4-ounce jelly jars, with about 1/2 cup left over

I adapted my mayapple marmalade recipe from Euell Gibbons' marmalade recipe in his classic book, *Stalking the Wild Asparagus*. Though Gibbons calls his recipe "marmalade," it fits the description of "jam" better, since it doesn't result in a product containing the bits of fruit and skin typical of marmalade. My modification produces a true marmalade. It is, however, extra work. If you're strapped for time or lack the energy or ambition, follow his recipe (or, follow my recipe, skipping the 2nd and 3rd sentences of step 2, and all of steps 3 and 4). You'll still wind up with a fragrant and flavorful product.

Caution: Use only ripe mayapples; the green, unripe fruit is toxic. Ripe mayapples have no hint of green in them at all (green indicates toxicity). When ripe, they range from creamy white to yellowish white to lemon yellow in color, and they are soft. Any of these colors is fine for marmalade. Discard translucent mayapples and trim off large brown or black rotten spots. Their off-flavor detracts from the rest of the batch.

THE RECIPE

2 heaping quarts ripe mayapples (review the Caution)

1 cup water

5 cups sugar

1 box fruit pectin (like Sure-Jell®)

Six 8-ounce or twelve 4-ounce jelly jars with new lids and rings – washed, rinsed and sterilized (see page 175 for how to sterilize glass jars). The lids and rings should be kept on the stove in a pot of very hot water, but there is no need to boil them. The glass jars, however, should be filled with water and submerged in a pot deep enough to cover them with the water brought to a boil.

1. Gently rinse the mayapples in cold water to remove any dirt and to surprise any critters that you may have collected along with the mayapples.

2. Remove the stem end and blossom ends, then quarter the fruit. During this process, visually inspect each mayapple, setting aside two heaping cups' worth of quarters from the nicest looking specimens. (They will be cut up and used for the fruit pieces that distinguish marmalade from jelly and jam.) Put the rest of the quarters in a large, tall pot.

3. Now take the two cups of quarters that you set aside, and scoop out the clear, jelly-like pulp with seeds. Add the pulp and seeds to the large pot. As you do this, you'll notice that there is a thin membrane between the soft flesh and the jelly-like pulp. This membrane should be removed and dropped into the pot along with the pulp, or it will interfere with cutting the segments into smaller pieces in the next step. Most of the time you'll be able to scoop it out along with the jelly-like pulp and seeds; occasionally, you'll have to peel it off separately.

4. Using a very sharp knife or scissors, cut the soft fruit segments into smaller pieces and set them aside.

5. Add a cup of water to the large pot containing the pulp. Cover and simmer for 15 minutes, stirring occasionally to prevent sticking.

6. After the pulp has simmered for 15 minutes, it can be gently mashed and put through a colander or Foley food mill to remove the seeds (considered poisonous) and skins (a textural nuisance.)

7. To the strained pulp, add the cut-up pieces from step 4. Stir. (This mixture should equal 4 cups. If it doesn't, make up the difference with water.) Pour it back into the large pot, stir in the box of Sure-Jell and bring it to a boil. Immediately add 5 cups of sugar. Stir. (While this is coming to a boil, use canning jar tongs to empty the hot water out of the sterilized jelly jars and pour it back into the pot of jars and water. Set the empty sterilized jars on a cooling rack.) Bring the marmalade to a hard, rolling boil, and stirring constantly, boil for one minute. Go immediately to step 8.

8. Quickly pour the marmalade into the sterilized jelly jars, filling each to within a quarter of an inch from the top. (I find that a Pyrex™ glass measuring cup with a pouring spout works nicely for the transfer.) Wipe the jar rims and threads with a clean dishcloth dipped in water from the jar sterilizing pot. Cover promptly with a lid taken from the pot of very hot water. Screw the bands on tightly. (There should be about half a cup of marmalade left to refrigerate in a margarine tub or extra jelly jar. Pour and scrape it out of the pot before it has time to set. I love having this for breakfast on toast or a toasted English muffin or crumpet.)

9. Check the seals a couple of hours later, after the jars have cooled, by pressing down on the center of the lid. If the lid cannot be depressed, a good seal has been made. Refrigerate any jars that did not seal, and use them first.

NOTE:

Once upon a time, trying to double or halve jelly, jam or marmalade recipes was a waste of time and effort. It didn't work. Now, you can buy a 4.7 ounce container of Ball® RealFruit™ Classic Pectin, and make as little as 2 half-pints or as many as 10 half-pints at a time following instructions under the peel-off label. For 2 jars, you'd only need 1-1/3 cups of mayapple fruit prepared. That's a big help when mayapples aren't abundant.

– Thanks to Doug Mueller for this insight via Facebook.

Mulberry Taffy
Yield: 120-140 pieces

The inspiration for creating mulberry taffy came from Jim Meuninck and Jim Duke's *Edible Wild Plants: Video Field Guide to 100 Useful Wild Herbs*. In it, Jim M's young daughter has fun stretching and eating what he calls mulberry fudge. I've made his mulberry fudge before. It's good, but sticky, messy to eat, and a bear to clean up. After several failed tries at making taffy, I searched the internet, and found a recipe for "Any Flavor Taffy," submitted by THE SCONE, on allrecipes.com. I replaced the water with mulberry juice, eliminated the package of unsweetened, fruit-flavored soft drink mix, and added vanilla and lemon juice, to give it a tad more flavor.

THE RECIPE:
2-1/2 cups white sugar
2 tablespoons butter
3 tablespoons cornstarch
1/2 teaspoon salt
1 cup corn syrup
2 tablespoons lemon juice
1-1/3 cups mulberry juice*
1 teaspoon vanilla

1. Butter and set aside two large baking sheets.
2. Stir together the sugar and cornstarch in a medium saucepan. Add the corn syrup, mulberry juice, butter and salt. Stir to blend. Insert a candy thermometer. Over medium heat, bring mixture to a boil, stirring occasionally so it doesn't stick to the bottom and burn. Cook until the mixture reads 250° F. Remove from heat and quickly pour onto the baking sheets. Let stand until cool enough to handle.

3. Butter the hands of helpers. Pull the taffy until it lightens in color and becomes stiffer. Roll into a rope about the thickness of your finger, and then cut into bite-size pieces 1–1-1/4" long. Wrap in 4" squares of waxed paper. (Don't substitute plastic wrap. Within 10 days, taffy wrapped in plastic wrap will dry to the point where it will crumble to powder when you bite into it and try to chew it.)

* *There are several ways that you can extract juice from the berries and also get rid of the tough little stems inside each fruit: cook them in a cup or two of water and pour the juice off; mash them and strain the pulpy juice through a cheesecloth or medium-fine sieve...or do as I do and use a Mehu-Liisa Finnish steam extractor (on Amazon for $100-plus). It will last for decades.*

Puffball Pieces

There is nothing quite like the experience of finding your first giant puffball and harvesting it. But then what? Here is my recipe for delicious puffball pieces, battered and fried.

Before you start: Inspect the mushroom. Slice the puffball in half from top to bottom. (If there appears to be a stem and gills forming inside, it is not a puffball and you should dispose of the mushroom.) If you see any yellow, green or brown colors, or it smells putrid, the mushroom is too far gone to use. The inside should look like a marshmallow. Examine the outside skin carefully for tiny holes, which may indicate the presence of maggots inside the mushroom. If you find any holes, cut a slice of mushroom from below the holes and inspect. Unfortunately, the maggots are white, so they may be tough to spot unless they move. If you find any, dispose of the mushroom.

THE RECIPE:
Vegetable oil for frying
A giant puffball mushroom
Onion ring batter
Ranch dressing or honey barbecue sauce

1. Heat an electric skillet containing an inch of vegetable oil to 375° F. (Ours was 12" square and it took two quarts of vegetable oil.)
2. Cut the mushroom into small pieces approximately 2" square and 1/4" thick.
3. Dip the pieces into the onion ring batter. (We used Don's Chuckwagon Onion Ring Mix that we purchased at our local grocery store. All we had to add was water.)
4. Fry until light golden brown, and drain on paper towels.
5. Serve with ranch dressing or honey barbecue sauce on the side for dipping.

Shagbark Snickerdoodles
Yield: 42-48 Cookies

This is a modification of the snickerdoodles recipe on page 425 of *The Best Recipe*, by the editors of *Cook's Illustrated* magazine. The idea of adding shagbark hickory nuts is my own. I prefer a medium-sized cookie instead of a large cookie. It is less likely to break. For that reason, I changed the cookie dough ball to 1-1/4" in diameter instead of the 1-1/2" size in *The Best Recipe*. In the scores of batches made in my kitchen, I can usually count on getting 42–48 1-1/4" cookies. Of course, not all of them make it to the freezer. There's nothing quite like a few warm shagbark snickerdoodles and a glass of milk.

THE RECIPE:
2-1/4 cups all-purpose flour

1 teaspoon baking soda

2 teaspoons cream of tartar

1/2 teaspoon salt

1 cup shagbark hickory nuts, free of shell shards and chopped into medium-sized pieces

1-1/2 sticks softened, unsalted butter

1/4 cup vegetable shortening

2 large eggs

1-1/2 cups granulated sugar

3 tablespoons sugar & 1 tablespoon ground cinnamon, mixed, for rolling cookies

1. Set oven rack in middle position and preheat oven to 400° F. Grease three cookie sheets or line them with parchment paper and set aside.

2. In a medium bowl, whisk together flour, baking soda, cream of tartar and salt. Add hickory nuts to the mixture, whisking to distribute. Set aside.

3. In another bowl, mix together the butter, shortening and sugar until combined. Use a rubber spatula to scrape down the sides of the bowl. Add in eggs. Beat 30 seconds with an electric mixer at medium speed, or by hand.

4. Add dry ingredients from bowl in step 2 and beat at low speed for 20 seconds.

5. Working with about 2 tablespoons of dough each time, roll the dough into 1-1/4" balls. Roll balls in the cinnamon-sugar mix and place them about 2–2-1/2" apart on the cookie sheets.

6. Bake one sheet at a time for 9–11 minutes or until the edges of the cookies are beginning to set and the centers are soft and puffy.

7. Let cookies cool on the cookie sheet a few minutes before moving them to a cooling rack with a wide spatula. Once cool, transfer snickerdoodles to a lidded plastic container, separating the layers with waxed paper. Store in the freezer. They will keep up to six months unless you have a Cookie Monster in your house like I do!

NOTES:

Tested Vegan Alternative: in place of butter, use 1-1/2 sticks of Fleischmann's unsalted margarine. In place of 2 eggs, mix 2 tablespoons of milled flax seed with 6 tablespoons of water.

ShagBARK Syrup
Yield: 2¼ pints

BARK is capitalized for emphasis. This syrup is NOT made by boiling down the sap of the tree, like many other types of syrups in the spring of the year. Instead, the secret lies in extracting flavor and color from strips of the shaggy bark. While I've had success making it in the fall, winter and spring, I believe that summer would work just as well. The resultant syrup has a pleasant "hickory smoked" flavor, making it a tasty treat for any breakfast-themed meal.

THE RECIPE:
10.5 ounces shagbark hickory tree bark,
  broken into small strips (measured on a kitchen scale)
2 quarts water
2 cups sugar
2 cups brown sugar

1. Begin by picking a handful of bark strips from a shagbark hickory tree *(Carya ovata)*, being sure that the pieces have the reddish-brown part found on the bark's underside. (I believe that it is the source of the flavor and the color.) Rinse any dust and critters off. Break the strips into shorter pieces so that they will fit into the bottom of your pot.

2. Place bark pieces in a pot and add the water. Cover and bring to a boil, then reduce heat and simmer for 20 minutes. Remove the bark. Filter the extract through a cloth into a bowl. You should end up with approximately 2 cups of bark extract.

3. Pour the extract back into the clean pot and add the plain and brown sugars. Heat and stir until all the sugar has dissolved.

4. Pour into two sterilized pint jars to within 1/2" of the top. Cover with a lid and screw down the ring. Process the jars in a boiling water bath for 10 minutes.

NOTES:
Credit for the idea: During my wild foods session at the 2009 Midwest Environmental Education Conference in Illinois, Cliff Knapp shared a story of how outdoor education legend L.B. Sharp made shagbark syrup. Intrigued, but with no ingredient amounts to go by, I decided to try it. The amounts I used above worked beautifully, producing a couple of pints plus some to use on pancakes or French toast or waffles or ice cream right away.

Sumac Lemonade – Two Ways

Yield: 3 quarts for each recipe

Students in my 7th grade science classes learned experimenting skills by trying to find the answer to this question: "How can we produce consistently good looking and good tasting sumac lemonade?" After 20 years of research and testing, we concluded that the two recipes below produced sumac lemonade that was consistently equal in appearance and taste.

GIANT TEA BAG METHOD*
1 quart super-sour, bright red sumac drupes
1-1/2 quarts of boiling water
3/4 cup sugar (or sweeten to taste)
4 pounds of ice

TOOLS:
Cheesecloth and scissors
Large rubber band
Long wooden spoon
Tongs
1-gallon plastic pitcher

1. Cut two rectangular pieces of cheesecloth 24-30" long. Lay one on top of the other, crisscrossing at right angles.

2. Put the drupes in the middle, and then bring up the sides and twist, forming a giant tea bag. Fold the top over and secure it with a rubber band.

3. Put the tea bag in a gallon pitcher with the top of the bag sticking up. Pour the boiling water over the tea bag. Use the tongs to dunk the bag up and down for no more than 10 seconds. Let it drain into the pitcher, then dispose of the bag.

4. Stir in sugar until dissolved. Add ice to bring the level to 3 quarts. Taste. Add more sugar if necessary.

Credit for the idea of forming a giant tea bag belongs to Jim Meuninck. He demonstrated it in a video he did with James Duke, titled Edible Wild Plants Video Field Guide to 100 Useful Wild Herbs, Media Methods, 24097 North Shore Drive, Edwardsburg, MI 49112.

TWO-MINUTE STIR METHOD
1 quart super-sour, bright red sumac drupes
3 quarts cold water
¾ cup sugar

TOOLS:
Two 1-gallon plastic pitchers
Long wooden spoon
Flour sack dishtowel

1. Place the drupes in one pitcher and add 3 quarts of water.

2. Stir with a wooden spoon for two minutes.

3. Place a flour sack dishtowel over the other pitcher, letting it sag into the pitcher a little bit. Have a helper hold it in place so it can't slip down, as you pour the liquid out of the stirred pitcher. This removes the drupes and sediment. Carefully lift the towel off and dispose of it with the drupes and sediment.

4. Stir in the sugar and taste. Add more sugar if necessary.

Wild Food Trail Bites

Gluten Free
Yield: 12-20, depending on
how many ingredients you add

This is a high-energy snack to carry along when you go hiking, or just to nibble on when you need a "boost." When I lived in Michigan, our Scout troop enjoyed the Council's annual winter hike along the Potawatomi Trail. We once encountered a Scout carrying a big bowl under his arm. He explained that it was a mix of peanut butter, dry milk powder and honey. He liked it so much that he brought enough to share with other Scouts he met along the trail. While the concoction seemed strange to us, we had to admit that it tasted pretty good. As we continued hiking, we could also tell that it was providing us with extra energy. For years afterwards, we often made a similar version to take with us on our winter hikes, along with our own version of GORP (Good Old Raisins and Peanuts and M&Ms.)

THE RECIPE

1 cup or a little more of powdered milk

1/2 cup wildflower honey

*1/3 cup each of rolled oats; coarsely chopped hazelnuts, hickory nuts, black walnuts and Missouri northern pecans; medium to finely chopped apricots; and sweetened, shredded coconut

1/4 cup peanut butter

1/4 cup persimmon pulp or wild plum jam

---

* Not every item is necessary; substitutions can be made, such as amaranth seed and lambsquarters seed.

1. Knead all ingredients together with your hands, adding more powdered milk if necessary. The right consistency will be a stiff, but not crumbly, dough. Shape into logs about an inch in diameter and cut into 1–3" pieces. Roll in powdered milk, shredded coconut or powdered sugar.

NOTES:
This is a greatly modified version of the POW Bars recipe found
in *Backpacker's Cookbook*, by Margaret Cross and Jean Fiske.
I suspect it was the source of the recipe used by the Scout we met
on the trail decades ago. Using it as a springboard, I provided
a variety of wild ingredients, and my housekeeper, Mary Frakes,
used her creativity to produce three different versions, varying
from five to seven wild items. We liked the one above best, and
I entered it in the Hazel Wood Commemorative Wild Foods
Contest at the annual Cairo, WV, Nature Wonder Wild Foods
Weekend one September. Mary's entry won first place for the best
wild food dish.

Feel free to experiment and use what you have in the way of
wild ingredients. Mulberries are good, and so are serviceberries,
wild black raspberries, blueberries and red raspberries. Raisins
and Craisins (dried cranberries) are fine. However, I prefer
mulberries that were frozen instead of mulberries that were dried.
Applesauce could be used in place of persimmon pulp.

Wild Grape Popsicles

*Yield: 14–16 popsicles, depending on
the number of cells in the ice cube tray*

'Tis said that one of America's first names was Vinland, as an
abundance of vines greeted the explorers who landed on her
shores. Wild grapes might well have been the dominant vine.
Wild grapes are pea-sized versions of table grapes. My students
had two favorite ways to enjoy them: one was as wild grape jelly
(every bit as good as Concord grape jelly); the other, as wild grape
popsicles.

THE RECIPE
For each ice cube tray that you plan to fill, you'll want:
1 cup ripe wild grapes, rinsed and picked free from their stems
2 cups water
2 tablespoons sugar

TOOLS:
Ice cube tray(s)
**Cardboard to cover
  the tray (see photo)**
Craft sticks

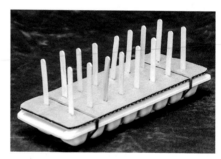

1. Put the grapes and
   water in a pot. Do
   not mash the grapes.

2. Heat until boiling, then turn the heat down to low. Cover and
   simmer for 20 minutes.

3. Strain the juice through a cloth into a bowl. Discard the grapes,
   and pour the juice back in the pot.

4. Add the sugar. Heat and stir until the sugar is dissolved. Add
   more sugar to taste. Let the juice cool while you make a
   cardboard cover for your ice cube tray, as shown.

Purple tongues! Whitmore Lake Middle School 7th graders Nicole Salamin and Jessica Garrett check their tongues while eating wild grape popsicles.

5. Remove the cover and fill the tray with wild grape juice. Replace the cover and hold it in place with rubber bands. Insert the craft sticks.

6. Freeze overnight.

NOTES:

Tip: clean up spills with a wet dishrag; remove stains with diluted liquid chlorine bleach.

Credit for determining the amounts of wild grapes, water and sugar to use to make a tray of wild grape popsicles belongs to Jessica Garrett. Jessica was a student in my 7th grade science class at Whitmore Lake Middle School, in Whitmore Lake, MI, and took on the challenge for extra credit. Advice on using a cardboard cover to support the craft sticks came from Louise Smitter, a wonderful lady who served as a cook for the school.

Glossary

Alluvial: refers to the soil in a flood plain habitat. Imagine hard rains and rapidly running water washing away soil from farms and carrying it downstream. Soon, there is more water than the stream banks can hold and it floods over the adjacent land. Over time, the level of the stream drops, and parts of the area still hold water. Slowly, the soil that water was carrying settles out on top of the ground. This is known as alluvial soil. Silver maple is one of the trees that can survive occasional flooding. It grows well on alluvial soils.

Astringent: makes your mouth feel dry

Awn: a small, pointed covering over a seed; it may end in a stiff bristle. Commonly seen in grasses and grains such as wheat, oats, and rye, and also found in amaranth. These are unpleasant if they get inside your mouth, so they need to be winnowed out.

Axil: a small area of the stem immediately above where a leaf is attached; the upper angle between a leafstalk or a branch and the supporting stem

Axillary: term for a cluster of leaves that grow out from the axil above an older leaf or branch. Axillary leaves of lambsquarters are younger and more tender than the leaves below.

Basal Rosette: a term given to describe leaves that grow outwards from the bottom of a plant. This pattern resembles the petals of a rose flower. They are all attached to the center, and grow outwards.

Berry: a fruit whose multiple, unprotected seeds are surrounded by flesh. (An unprotected seed does not have any covering over it, like the hard shell found inside apricots, peaches and plums.) The fruit is typically juicy when ripe. Examples include blueberries and huckleberries, mayapples and wild grapes. Tomatoes are berries.

Blanch: to prepare for freezing by immersing briefly in boiling water. This stops the action of enzymes and helps retain fresh bright colors.

Bract: the part of a flower immediately below the blossom. In a dandelion, the flower is yellow, and the bract below it is green (and very bitter tasting.)

Calyx: the collective name given sepals, which are the flower parts immediately under the petals. The calyx forms the outside protective covering of a flower bud. When persimmon fruits ripen and become soft, the 4-to-5-pointed calyx may be seen clinging to the fruit. It resembles a stiff, tough, dark brown star. If it can be easily twisted off, the persimmon is ready to eat; if it is still tightly attached to the fruit, the persimmon will make your mouth pucker up.

Cap: the top of a mushroom that has a shape similar to the button, crimini or portabella mushrooms sold in stores.

Clonal: a group of plants that originate from one individual that spreads underground. Sumac is an example of a clonal group.

Compound Drupe: a fruit that consists of several connected drupes, such as blackberries, black raspberries, and mulberries

Compound Leaf: a leaf made up of three or more leaflets

Coniferous: a cone-bearing tree or shrub, typically with needle-like leaves. Some are evergreen, like fir, pine, and spruce, and don't shed all of their needles at once; others have needle-like leaves that turn yellow to brown in the fall and are replaced in the spring with new growth, like bald cypress and larch

Deciduous: a tree that sheds its leaves in the fall and has them replaced by new leaves in the spring

Drupe: a fruit whose one seed is encased inside a tough shell, such as a cherry, peach, apricot or plum. A berry (see *Berry*) has several seeds with no shell, such as a blueberry or a tomato. Drupes may have a fleshy covering, as in a cherry, or have a very thin, dry skin, as in sumac, basswood, and hackberry.

Emergent Aquatic Plant: a plant capable of living with its roots under water, while growing with most of its leaves out of water; cattail is an example

Fairy Ring: a dark green ring in the grass caused by mushrooms that grow there. The mushrooms help absorb water and break down organic materials and minerals in the soil, making nitrogen, phosphorus and potassium (major ingredients in fertilizer) available to the grass. With the extra nitrogen and water, the grass turns darker green than the surrounding grass. Several species of mushrooms can form a fairy ring. Some are edible; others are poisonous.

Flaccid: soft and limp. Said of a leaf that it is beginning to wilt from lack of water.

Flesh: another name for the edible tissue of a mushroom or plant

Forage: to hunt for and collect edible wild plants and mushrooms

Gill: thin, flexible, blade-like tissue under the cap of a mushroom that produces spores. The gills of a mushroom are perpendicular to the cap, attached to it, and run from the stipe (see *Stipe*) to the outer margin of the cap. They are arranged in a radial pattern like the spokes of a bicycle wheel.

Husk: 1) the fleshy covering of some nuts, such as black walnut or shagbark hickory;

2) a thin, leaf-like covering over the flowering spike of cattail, like the husk over an ear of corn, but thinner

Key (as in the silver maple key): a combination of a seed case and a samara (a winged structure that helps the seed spread to a new location when the wind blows)

Key Out: to identify with a reference book; to identify by answering a succession of yes or no questions based on observable characteristics

Leaching: to remove bitter-tasting tannins from acorns by rinsing the acorns repeatedly with water

Leaflet: one part of a compound leaf

Lenticel: a corky dot or dash visible on the bark of a plant stem. It functions for gas exchange during photosynthesis before the leaves appear.

Lobe: a leaf blade projection. Lobes of the white oak group of trees tend to be rounded; lobes of the red oak group tend to be pointed.

Margin: the edge of a leaf; the edge of a mushroom cap

Midvein: short for the middle vein of a leaf. Except when the leaf has parallel venation, it is the largest of the veins visible on the underside of the leaf. In addition to supplying water from the roots through the smaller branching veins to the cells that carry on photosynthesis and sending glucose back, the midvein's structure helps support the leaf.

Mushroom: the common name given the fruiting body of a fungus. "Toadstool" was once reserved for poisonous fungi, and "mushroom" was assigned to all edible fungi. "Toadstool" is no longer used. As to mushrooms, there are poisonous mushrooms and edible mushrooms.

Nutmeat: the edible part inside the hard shelled nut

Nutpick: a pointed metal tool that is used to free pieces of nutmeat from the cracked shell

Pappus: a very-fine, lightweight hair structure that aids in the dispersal of seeds by the wind. Dandelion seeds have them; so does milkweed and cattail.

Pedicel: the stem that holds a fruit

Petiole: a leaf's stem or stalk that attaches it to the plant

Pinnately compound leaf: a leaf with its leaflets attached to the sides of a central leaf stalk, such as the leaf of black walnut or sumac

Pubescence: very fine, short hairs that cover the surface of a leaf, stem or drupe

Polypore: a group of mushrooms easily recognized by the many tiny pinholes on the underside of the cap. The reproductive spores drop from these holes.

Potherb: a plant whose leaves, stems, flower buds or flowers are cooked and eaten, or a plant used as a seasoning.

Raceme: a type of flower head that resembles a bottlebrush – the flowers grow along the length of a central flowering stalk without branching

Receptacle: the end portion of a stem around which a compound fruit is formed. When a blackberry is picked, the receptacle comes off with the fruit and can be seen as a light colored and somewhat woody plug or core. Picking a black raspberry, however, leaves the receptacle on the plant. The fruit appears to be hollow, like a thimble.

Rhizome: an underground starch storage organ of a plant such as a cattail. It starts below the soil surface at the base of a plant. It runs horizontally away from the plant. A few roots may be attached to it. At the growing end, a white, sharply-pointed lateral shoot pushes its way through the soil. It may turn upwards and produce a new plant.

Runners, underground: one of the ways that a plant spreads is by underground runners. These are specialized roots (rhizomes) or stolons (stems), often near the surface, from which new plants will grow. As this is a type of vegetative reproduction, the plants produced this way are said to be clonal (genetically identical.) Sumac is a good example. The clones are either female or male. The female clonal stands have red fruit heads; the males don't.

Samara: a dry, indehiscent, winged fruit. "Indehiscent" means that it doesn't split. The wings are an adaptation that helps the seeds get distributed by the wind. Examples in this guide include the samaras (also known as keys) of silver maple, which spin like helicopter blades as they drop from the tree, and the wafer-like samaras of Siberian elm.

Scientific name: a name that identifies an individual living (or once living) thing. The full set of names for an individual includes its kingdom, phylum, class, order, family, genus and species. This, however, is cumbersome. In practice, only the genus and species are used when one refers to a plant or a mushroom by its scientific name. The genus name always comes first and is capitalized and italicized. The species name follows. It is never capitalized, but it is always italicized. Most scientific names are in Latin, a "dead language" whose meanings do not change.

Scientific names are the same around the world and are preferred for accuracy when seeking to learn if a mushroom or a plant is reported as edible, inedible, or poisonous. Common names can be misleading. The same common name may be given to totally different plants or mushrooms.

Shoot: the tip of new plant growth. An asparagus shoot is a good example. Cattails have lateral shoots which grow away from the parent plant to start another. These lateral shoots can be cooked and eaten.

Skirt, rolled: this term is used to describe the margin of a young chanterelle mushroom cap. Its outer edge is folded or rolled over, and is slightly wavy at the bottom.

sp.: abbreviation used when referring to a single species. There are several red-capped, white mushrooms growing in my front yard. They have the appearance and characteristics of the Russula genus. Until I can key them out with reference books, I will label them in my refrigerator as Russula sp.

Spike: a very narrow type of flowering structure. Plantain has flower spikes; so does cattail.

Spore: the reproductive cell of a mushroom

Spore print: the deposit left behind when a mushroom cap is placed face down on a piece of paper and left for several hours or overnight. As there are light-colored spores or dark-colored spores, standard practice is to set the mushroom half on a black piece of paper and half on a white piece of paper. The color of the deposit (spore color) is one of the characteristics used to help identify mushrooms.

spp.: abbreviation meaning "several species." *Rubus* for instance, is the genus name for over 600 species of thorny plants that occur from coast to coast in the US and Canada. They include the vine-like trailing dewberries and the bush-like blackberries, raspberries, and thimbleberries. If I wanted to refer to the whole group or to the many that might be found in my state, I might write "*Rubus* spp." To refer to a specific one of them, I would use its scientific name. *Rubus occidentalis*, for instance, is black raspberry.

Stamen: the male reproductive part of a flower; its tip has pollen cells

Starch storage organ: sugars produced by photosynthesis in the leaves are stored as starches in the roots or rhizomes. The cattail stores its starches in a rhizome.

Stemlet: a short stem that holds an individual fruit in a cluster, such as the stemlets in a fruit head of sumac; these might also be called pedicels

Succulent: a plant that has a thick, fleshy stem and thick, fleshy leaves. These adaptations help it survive in dry environments.

Stipe: the stalk or stem of a mushroom

Tannins: bitter-tasting compounds found in acorns, autumn olives, the base of plantain leaves and petioles, sumac seeds, and grape seeds

Taproot: a large, central root that goes straight down. It may store energy, as does a carrot.

Tart: agreeably sour

Processing Tips

STERILIZING GLASS CANNING JARS

Canning is a time-honored way of preserving foods to eat later. Since the glass jars and the food that they contain will be stored at room temperature, it is imperative that the jars be sterilized before the hot cooked food or jelly is ladled into them and they are sealed. Otherwise, bacteria or mold can ruin your efforts. While there is only one recipe in this book that involves canning (mayapple marmalade), the canning process could also be used for microwaved purslane pickles, wild grape jelly, wild plums, and wild plum jam. You should be able to find recipes for the last three on the internet.

- Wash the jars, lids and rings in hot, soapy water. Rinse thoroughly. (Or, do in a dishwasher.)

- Fill the jars with water. Set them inside a kettle and cover them with water. Put a lid on the kettle and heat the water to boiling. Boil for 10 minutes, then turn off the heat and leave the kettle covered and on the burner.

- Simmer lids and rings separately for 10 minutes (a magnetic lid lifter easily plucks the lids and rings from the water, when it is time to use them.) Turn off the burner and leave them in the hot water until then.

- Empty the water out of the sterilized jars (a vinyl-coated jar lifter is the tool of choice for lifting the jars and pouring out the hot water; this and the magnetic lid lifter are likely to be found in hardware and grocery stores where canning supplies are sold.)

- Fill the sterilized jars with your jelly, jam or whatever else you intend to fill them with. Carefully wipe any food off the rim with a clean dishcloth that is moistened in the lids and rings pot of hot water. Seal them with the lids and rings.

- Check the seals a couple of hours later, after the jars have cooled, by pressing down on the center of the lid. If the lid cannot be depressed, a good seal has been made. Refrigerate any jars that did not seal and use them first.

VACUUM SEALING

You can vacuum seal a bag using a vacuum sealer machine or by using this method:*

How to vacuum seal without a machine:

- Wash your food. Remove any unwanted leaves, etc.
- Grab a re-sealable plastic bag.
- Put the food in the bag and seal the bag, leaving an approximately one-inch opening
- Lower the bag with the food in it into a bowl of water (sealed end up, of course)
- As you lower the bag into the water, the pressure of the water will force all of the air out of the bag. As you are doing this, you may need to move the bag around a bit to make sure you get all the air out. Be sure to not get water in the bag.
- After all the air is out, seal the bag while it is still in the water.
- Place your vacuum sealed food in the freezer to preserve it.

*source: http://www.foodandwine.com/blogs/low-tech-diy-way-vacuum-seal-your-food

DOUBLE BAGGING

Pawpaws become bitter over time due to oxidation. To make frozen pawpaw pulp last longer, Kathy Dice recommends double bagging. (Kathy and her husband Tom Wahl operate Red Fern Farm, in Wapello, Iowa, which has a u-pick for pawpaws, chestnuts, and persimmons.) Double bagging is exactly what it sounds like: protecting the food inside two plastic bags. Begin with a heavy-duty freezer bag, add the pawpaw pulp, and vacuum-seal it. Label the second bag that will go over the first (it is easier to write on it when it is empty), then slip it over the first bag, and vacuum seal it to exclude all air. If you don't have a vacuum-sealing machine, the low-tech way to vacuum seal your food works surprisingly well.

Recommendations for Learning More

FORAGING INSTRUCTORS

http://www.eattheweeds.com/foraging/foraging-instructors/

OUTSTANDING BOOKS ON FORAGING

Sam Thayer, *The Forager's Harvest: A Guide to Identifying, Harvesting, and Preparing Edible Wild Plants*, 2006, and *Nature's Garden: A Guide to Identifying, Harvesting, and Preparing Edible Wild Plants*, 2010. (Forager's Harvest, 528 W. Railroad Ave., Bruce, WI 54819)

Dr. John Kallas, *Edible Wild Plants: Wild Foods from Dirt to Plate*, 2010. (Gibbs-Smith, Layton, UT)

Ellen Zachos, *Backyard Foraging: 65 Familiar Plants You Didn't Know You Could Eat*, 2013. (Storey Publishing, North Adams, MA)

Mark Vorderbruggen, *IDIOT'S Guides: Foraging*, 2015.

Lee Peterson, *A Field Guide to Edible Wild Plants of Eastern and Central North America*, 1977 (Houghton Mifflin, Boston, MA)

Leda Meredith, *Northeast Foraging: 120 wild and flavorful edibles from beach plums to wineberries*, 2014 (Timber Press, Portland, OR.) Others in the Timber Press series, with the same format, are Douglas Deur's *Pacific Northwest Foraging*, Lisa Rose's *Midwest Foraging*, Judith Lowry's *California Foraging*, Chris Bennett's *Southeast Foraging*, and Briana Wiles' *Mountain States Foraging*. This website lists the states each book covers when you click on its name: www.timberpress.com/search/foraging.

Leda Meredith, *The Forager's Feast: How to Identify, Gather, and Prepare Wild Edibles*, 2016 (The Countryman Press, New York)

"Wildman" Steve Brill, *Identifying and Harvesting Edible and Medicinal Plants in Wild and Not So Wild Places*, 1994 (William Morrow/Harper Collins, New York)

"Wildman" Steve Brill, *Foraging with Kids: A Teacher's, Parent's, and Grandparent's Guide to Edible Wild Plants and Mushrooms*, 2014. Published by the author. Available from http://www.wildmanstevebrill.com.

Christopher Nyerges, *Foraging Wild Edible Plants of North America: More than 150 Delicious Recipes Using Nature's Edibles*, 2016 (Falcon Guides, Guilford, CT)

Dina Falconi and Wendy Hollender, *Foraging & Feasting: A Field Guide and Wild Food Cookbook*, 2013. (Botanical Arts Press, Accord, NY)

FAVORITE WILD FOODS COOKBOOK/ BERRIES & FRUITS FIELD GUIDES

Teresa Marrone's *Abundantly Wild: Collecting and Cooking Wild Edibles in the Upper Midwest*. 2004 (Adventure Publications, Cambridge, MN)

Teresa's wild berries and fruits field guide series may eventually cover our whole country. These four are in print now: *Wild Berries & Fruits Field Guide to Minnesota, Wisconsin and Michigan*, the *Wild Berries & Fruits Field Guide to Illinois, Iowa and Missouri*, the *Wild Berries & Fruits Field Guide to Ohio, Indiana and Kentucky*, and the *Wild Berries & Fruits Field Guide to the Rocky Mountains States*. Each has a companion cookbook with company-pleasing recipes. The spiral-bound binding is preferable as it allows the book to stay open when following a recipe.

IMPRESSIVE MUSHROOM REFERENCES

Dennis Desjardin, Michael Wood and Frederick Stevens. *California Mushrooms: The Comprehensive Identification Guide*, 2015 (Timber Press, Portland, OR)

Teresa Marrone and Kathy Yerich. *Mushrooms of the Upper Midwest*, 2014 (Adventure Publications, Cambridge, MN)

Joe McFarland and Greg Mueller. *Edible Wild Mushrooms of Illinois & Surrounding States*, 2009 (University of Illinois Press, Champaign-Urbana)

Michael Kuo, *100 Edible Mushrooms With Tested Recipes*, 2007 (University of Michigan Press, Ann Arbor)

John Plischke III, *Good Mushroom, Bad Mushroom: Who's Who, Where to Find Them, and How to Enjoy Them Safely, (All You Need to Know About the Mushrooms of North America)*, 2011 (St. Lynn's Press, Pittsburgh, PA)

Gary Lincoff, *The Complete Mushroom Hunter: An Illustrated Guide to Finding, Harvesting, and Enjoying Wild Mushrooms.* 2010 (Quarry Books, Beverly, MA)

Peter Jordan and Steven Wheeler, *The Complete Book of Mushrooms: An Illustrated Encyclopedia of Edible Mushrooms and over 100 Delicious Ways to Cook Them, With Over 800 Colour Photographs.* 2011 ed. (Southwater, UK)

LEARNING FROM OTHERS

North Carolina Wild Food Weekend, Betsy-Jeff Penn 4H Center, Reidsville, NC. This event, the second oldest in the U.S., is held on the third full weekend in April. For registration information, check the Facebook group page: NC Wildfood Weekend.

Midwest Wild Harvest Festival, Wisconsin Badger Camp, 10 miles south of Prairie du Chien, in SW WI. Held annually on the second weekend of September. http://wildharvestfestival.org

Nature Wonder Wild Foods Weekend, North Bend State Park, Cairo, West Virginia. Held annually on the third full weekend of September. Grandmother of all wild food weekends. http://www.wildfoodadventures.com/naturewonderweekend.html

MUSHROOM HUNTING CLUBS

North American mushroom clubs can be found in most states, six Canadian Provinces, and Mexico. Go to this website for details: http://www.namyco.org/clubs/index.html.

WILD EDIBLE WEBSITES

http://foraging.com
http://www.wildfoodadventures.com
http://rosesprodigalgarden.org
http://www.foragersharvest.com
http://www.wildmanstevebrill.com
http://www.eattheweeds.com

APPS FOR SMART PHONES

Wild Edibles. WinterRoot LLC. "Wildman" Steve Brill, Becky Lerner, Christopher Nyerges

Wild Edibles Lite. WinterRoot LLC. "Wildman" Steve Brill.

Wild Edibles App. RawFamily.com. Sergei Boutenko

STORES

Forager's Harvest
528 W Railroad Ave
Bruce, WI 54819
(715) 868-9453
http://foragersharvest.com

Hickory nut oil, fresh apples from no-spray orchard, Davebilt Nutcracker, Nut Wizards, many more essential foraging tools and outdoor books. Products like wild plum jam, wild grape jelly, and mayapple. Open Thurs.-Sat., 10 am – 6 pm.

Integration Acres Ltd.
9794 Chase Road, Albany, Ohio 45710
740-698-6060
info@integrationacres.com

Pawpaw and persimmon products

Nut Wizard® Store

Different sizes of Nut Wizards, with video demonstrations. Use this website to connect to the online store: http://www.nutwizard.com/prod01.htm. If you are within an easy drive of the store, however, you can save $12 to $18 shipping per Nut Wizard by driving to the store:

Seeds and Such, Inc.
1105 R Street, P.O. Box 81
Bedford, IN 47421
http://nutwizard@hpcisp.com
812-275-1016 local
888-321-9445 toll-free
Fax 812-275-4357

Photo Credits

All photos are by the author, except for the photos generously provided by the people named below:

Jace Stansbury – Fairy Ring/*Chlorophyllum Molybdites* - page xiv

Jim Frink, Prairie States Mushroom Club – Giant Puffball – page 88

Jeremy Moose Rappaport – Puffball Mushrooms – page 89

Jim Frink, Prairie States Mushroom Club – Hen of the Woods – page 91

Roger Heidt, Prairie States Mushroom Club – Common Yellow Morel, page 92

Roger Heidt, Prairie States Mushroom Club – Soil Temperature, page 93

Fred Stevens, Mykoweb.com – Oyster Mushroom – front cover and page 95

Jace Stansbury – Fairy Ring – page 96

Fred Stevens, Mykoweb.com – Scotch Bonnet – page 97

Jeni Reeves – White-Pored Sulfur Shelf – page 99

NOTE:
The following registered or trademarked products are mentioned in this book: Ball RealFruit Classic Pectin; Bisquick Baking Mix; Don's Chuckwagon Onion Ring Mix; Jiffy Mix; Mehu-Liisa; M&M's; Nut Wizard; Pillsbury; Sure-Jell

Index

Index

Index

Index

Acknowledgments

This book was made possible by the professionals at St. Lynn's Press, in Pittsburgh, Pennsylvania. Their experience in publishing, combined with their dedication, perseverance, patience and enthusiasm made it happen. My gratitude to them all: to Paul Kelly, the publisher and acquisitions editor; to Cathy Dees, the senior editor; to Holly Rosborough, art director; and to Chloe Wertz, who focuses on marketing and publicity. Thanks are also due to Morgan Stout, editorial intern, and Christina Gregory, publicity assistant. It was an honor to feel a part of the team.

Special thanks are due to Melissa Sokulski. A Pittsburgh-based forager, wild food educator and blogger with a big following and a full-time job, Melissa nevertheless took the time to serve as the technical editor on this book. Her insight caught mistakes that we were glad to correct before *The Scout's Guide* made it into print. Thanks also to Mississippi River Valley Council Scout Executive Todd Lamison for his insight on how the National Council of the Boy Scouts of America might feel about the title of the book, his advice and the contact information he provided for us to look into making the book available to Scouts and their leaders nationwide.

I am grateful to Glen Schwartz, Dean Abel, Roger Heidt, Dave Layton, and Damian Pieper – all members of the Prairie States Mushroom Club – for reviewing the mushroom accounts and offering photos. Jim Frink supplied several great photos.

Speaking of mushroom photos, a special thanks to Fred Stevens of Mykoweb.com for permission to use his superlative photo of *Pleurotus ostreatus*, the oyster mushroom. It is on the front cover and also on page 95. Jace Stansbury supplied a photo of a typical bright green ring left on grass by fairy ring mushrooms (page 96). Jeremy Moose Rappaport captured forager Andy Benson in a dilemma of what to do with all the giant puffball mushrooms he had collected (page 89.)

In addition to serving as my housekeeper, Mary Frakes has been a godsend with testing the activities and recipes that appear in this guide. She enjoys cooking and tasting wild foods. Mary also created two recipes that have won first place at the annual meeting of the National Wild Foods Association. One of them, Wild Food Trail Bites, is on page 162.

Many authors, wild food instructors, and researchers have contributed to what I know about identifying, collecting, processing, and storing edible wild plants and mushrooms. One of the most influential has been my good friend Sam Thayer. It is an honor to pass along what I have learned from Sam and from others.

Over a 50-year period, it has been a delight for me to share my enthusiasm for wild edibles with people of all ages. As a Scout leader, as a naturalist and nature centers director, as a middle school science teacher, and as a wild food instructor, it has been a rewarding experience. Thanks to all the young people who boldly went where they had never gone before, and had fun conducting scientific research on edible wild plants. Their enthusiasm made it fun for me to be part of the journey. Years later, it is a treat to have many of them as Facebook friends, and heartening to see their encouragement for this book.

I was blessed to have supportive school administrators during the 35 years that I was privileged to teach middle school science. They gave me the freedom to incorporate wild edibles into my electives and into my life science course.

Finally, without good friends and relatives to provide occasional breaks in routine and go out for a meal from time to time, the joy of writing might have become an ordeal. Thanks to my good friend and longtime colleague at Whitmore Lake, Michigan, Public Schools, Ron Bender, and to my brother Dan Krebill of Chapel Hill, North Carolina, for their generosity in hosting me.

OTHER BOOKS FROM ST. LYNN'S PRESS
www.stlynnspress.com

A Garden to Dye For
by Chris McLaughlin
160 pages • Hardback • ISBN: 978-0-9855622-8-1

Ramps
by the Editors of St. Lynn's Press
128 pages • Hardback • ISBN: 978-0-9832726-2-5

Good Mushroom Bad Mushroom
by John Plischke III
104 pages • Hardback • ISBN: 978-0-9819615-8-3

Good Berry Bad Berry
by Helen Yoest
112 pages • Hardback • ISBN: 978-1-9433660-1-9

About the Author

MIKE KREBILL is one of the Midwest's best-known foraging instructors and a member of the National Wild Foods Association Hall of Fame. Tens of thousands of people have joined him outdoors so that he could point out edible wild plants and mushrooms where they grow. Many people know Mike from his active participation in Facebook groups devoted to edible wild plants and mushrooms, where he shares his insights and enthusiasm.

Mike was an award-winning middle school science teacher for 35 years – Michigan Science Teacher of the Year, Michigan Environmental Educator of the Year, Keokuk (Iowa) Teacher of the Year – and before that, a naturalist and nature centers director for six years. Decades of experience with wild edibles have made him invaluable as a technical editor as well as a field guide author; he has served as the technical editor for nine wild edibles books and two manuscripts.

In a lifetime of devotion to Scouting, he has been active at every level, from Eagle Scout to Scoutmaster to leadership at the District and Council levels, receiving multiple honors for outstanding service. He was famous for taking his Scouts and students outdoors and for teaching science research skills by having them experiment with wild foods. His sumac lemonade, wild grape popsicles, and dandelion donuts were legendary.